M000099755

Simple
Baking

Irresistible, easy-to-follow recipes

Publications International, Ltd.

Let's get social!

@Publications_International
@PublicationsInternational
www.pilbooks.com

Table of Contents

Muffins, Biscuits & Scones

Orange Currant Scones

1½ cups all-purpose flour

¼ cup plus 1 teaspoon sugar, divided

1 teaspoon baking powder

¼ teaspoon salt

¼ teaspoon baking soda

⅓ cup currants

1 tablespoon grated orange peel

6 tablespoons (¾ stick) cold butter, cut into small pieces

½ cup buttermilk, yogurt or sour cream

1. Preheat oven to 425°F. Line baking sheet with parchment paper or spray with nonstick cooking spray.

2. Combine flour, ¼ cup sugar, baking powder, salt and baking soda in large bowl; mix well. Stir in currants and orange peel. Cut in butter with pastry blender or two knives until mixture resembles coarse crumbs. Add buttermilk; stir to form soft, sticky dough that clings together.

3. Shape dough into a ball; pat into 8-inch round on prepared baking sheet. Cut dough into eight wedges with floured knife. Sprinkle with remaining 1 teaspoon sugar.

4. Bake 18 to 20 minutes or until lightly browned. Remove to wire rack to cool 10 minutes.

Makes 8 scones

Classic Blueberry Muffins

1½ cups fresh or frozen
    blueberries
    (do not thaw)

2 cups all-purpose flour,
    divided

¾ cup sugar

2 teaspoons baking
    powder

½ teaspoon baking soda

½ teaspoon ground
    cinnamon

¼ teaspoon salt

    Dash ground nutmeg

¾ cup plus 2 tablespoons
    milk

½ cup (1 stick) butter,
    melted

1 egg

1 teaspoon vanilla

1. Preheat oven to 400°F. Line 15 standard (2½-inch) muffin cups with paper baking cups or spray with nonstick cooking spray.

2. Combine blueberries and 2 tablespoons flour in small bowl; toss to coat.

3. Combine remaining flour, sugar, baking powder, baking soda, cinnamon, salt and nutmeg in small bowl; mix well. Whisk milk, butter, egg and vanilla in medium bowl until well blended. Add to flour mixture; stir just until dry ingredients are moistened. Gently fold in blueberries. Spoon batter into prepared muffin cups, filling three-fourths full.

4. Bake 20 to 25 minutes or until toothpick inserted into centers comes out clean. Cool in pans 5 minutes; remove to wire racks. Serve warm or at room temperature.

Makes 15 muffins

Ham and Swiss Cheese Biscuits

2 cups all-purpose flour

2 teaspoons baking powder

½ teaspoon baking soda

¼ teaspoon salt

½ cup (1 stick) cold butter, cut into small pieces

⅔ cup buttermilk

½ cup (2 ounces) shredded Swiss cheese

2 ounces ham, finely chopped

1. Preheat oven to 450°F. Line baking sheet with parchment paper or spray with nonstick cooking spray.

2. Combine flour, baking powder, baking soda and salt in medium bowl; mix well. Cut in butter with pastry blender or two knives until mixture resembles coarse crumbs. Stir in buttermilk, 1 tablespoon at a time, until slightly sticky dough forms. Stir in cheese and ham.

3. Turn out dough onto lightly floured surface; knead lightly. Roll out dough to ½-inch thickness. Cut out biscuits with 2-inch biscuit or cookie cutter. Place 1 inch apart on prepared baking sheet.

4. Bake 10 minutes or until browned. Serve warm.

Makes about 18 biscuits

Apple Butter Spice Muffins

½ cup sugar

1 teaspoon ground cinnamon

¼ teaspoon ground nutmeg

⅛ teaspoon ground allspice

½ cup chopped pecans or walnuts

2 cups all-purpose flour

2 teaspoons baking powder

¼ teaspoon salt

1 cup milk

¼ cup vegetable oil

1 egg

¼ cup apple butter

1. Preheat oven to 400°F. Line 12 standard (2½-inch) muffin cups with paper baking cups or spray with nonstick cooking spray.

2. Combine sugar, cinnamon, nutmeg and allspice in large bowl. Remove 2 tablespoons sugar mixture to small bowl; toss with pecans until coated. Add flour, baking powder and salt to remaining sugar mixture; mix well.

3. Whisk milk, oil and egg in medium bowl until well blended. Add to flour mixture; stir just until dry ingredients are moistened. Spoon 1 tablespoon batter into each prepared muffin cup. Top with 1 teaspoon apple butter; spoon remaining batter evenly over apple butter. Sprinkle with pecan mixture.

4. Bake 20 to 25 minutes or until golden brown and toothpick inserted into centers comes out clean. Remove to wire rack to cool 10 minutes. Serve warm or cool completely.

Makes 12 muffins

Pumpkin Ginger Scones

½ cup sugar, divided

2 cups all-purpose flour

2 teaspoons baking powder

1 teaspoon ground cinnamon

½ teaspoon baking soda

½ teaspoon salt

¼ cup (½ stick) cold butter, cut into small pieces

1 egg

½ cup canned pumpkin

¼ cup sour cream

½ teaspoon grated fresh ginger *or* 2 tablespoons finely chopped crystallized ginger

1 tablespoon butter, melted

1. Preheat oven to 425°F.

2. Reserve 1 tablespoon sugar; set aside. Combine remaining sugar, flour, baking powder, cinnamon, baking soda and salt in large bowl; mix well. Cut in ¼ cup cold butter with pastry blender or two knives until mixture resembles coarse crumbs.

3. Whisk egg in medium bowl. Add pumpkin, sour cream and ginger; whisk until well blended. Add to flour mixture; stir to form soft dough that leaves side of bowl.

4. Turn out dough onto well floured surface; knead 10 times. Roll out dough into 9×6-inch rectangle with floured rolling pin. Cut into six 3-inch squares; cut each square diagonally in half to make 12 triangles. Place triangles 2 inches apart on ungreased baking sheets. Brush with 1 tablespoon melted butter; sprinkle with reserved sugar.

5. Bake 10 to 12 minutes or until golden brown. Remove to wire rack to cool 10 minutes. Serve warm.

Makes 12 scones

Chile Pecan Biscuits

½ cup (1 stick) cold butter, divided

2 tablespoons jalapeño pepper,* minced (about 1 large)

⅓ cup finely chopped pecans

1 tablespoon honey

2 cups all-purpose flour

1 tablespoon baking powder

½ teaspoon salt

⅛ teaspoon chipotle chili powder

¼ teaspoon ground cumin

¾ cup milk

5 tablespoons shredded sharp Cheddar cheese (optional)

Jalapeño peppers can sting and irritate the skin, so wear rubber gloves when handling, and do not touch your eyes.

1. Preheat oven to 425°F. Line baking sheet with parchment paper or spray with nonstick cooking spray.

2. Melt 1 tablespoon butter in small skillet over medium heat. Add jalapeño and pecans; cook and stir 3 to 5 minutes or until jalapeño is tender and pecans are fragrant. Stir in honey; set aside to cool.

3. Combine flour, baking powder, salt, chili powder and cumin in large bowl; mix well. Cut remaining 7 tablespoons butter into small pieces. Cut butter into flour mixture with pastry blender or two knives until mixture resembles small chunks. Stir in pecan mixture and milk; knead gently to form dough.

4. Turn out dough onto lightly floured surface; pat to ¾-inch thickness. Cut out biscuits with 2½-inch biscuit or cookie cutter. Place 1 inch apart on prepared baking sheet. Pat about 1½ teaspoons cheese onto each biscuit, if desired.

5. Bake 15 to 17 minutes or until golden brown. Remove to wire rack to cool slightly. Serve warm.

Makes 9 to 10 biscuits

Lemon Poppy Seed Muffins

2 cups all-purpose flour

1¼ cups granulated sugar

¼ cup poppy seeds

2 tablespoons plus 2 teaspoons grated lemon peel, divided

2 teaspoons baking powder

½ teaspoon baking soda

½ teaspoon ground cardamom

¼ teaspoon salt

2 eggs

½ cup (1 stick) butter, melted

½ cup milk

½ cup plus 2 tablespoons lemon juice, divided

1 cup powdered sugar

1. Preheat oven to 400°F. Line 18 standard (2½-inch) muffin cups with paper baking cups or spray with nonstick cooking spray.

2. Combine flour, granulated sugar, poppy seeds, 2 tablespoons lemon peel, baking powder, baking soda, cardamom and salt in large bowl; mix well.

3. Whisk eggs in medium bowl. Add butter, milk and ½ cup lemon juice; whisk until well blended. Add to flour mixture; stir just until blended. Spoon batter evenly into prepared muffin cups.

4. Bake 15 to 20 minutes or until toothpick inserted into centers comes out clean. Cool in pans on wire racks 10 minutes.

5. Meanwhile, prepare glaze. Combine powdered sugar and remaining 2 teaspoons lemon peel in small bowl; stir in enough remaining lemon juice to make pourable glaze. Place muffins on sheet of parchment or waxed paper; drizzle with glaze. Serve warm or at room temperature.

Makes 18 muffins

Peanut Butter and Jelly Monkey Biscuits

¼ cup creamy peanut butter

2 tablespoons butter

2¼ cups all-purpose flour

¼ cup sugar

1 tablespoon baking powder

½ teaspoon salt

¼ cup (½ stick) cold butter, cut into small pieces

¾ cup buttermilk

6 tablespoons seedless strawberry jam, or favorite flavor

1. Preheat oven to 350°F. Line 9×5-inch loaf pan with foil, leaving 2-inch overhang. Spray foil with nonstick cooking spray.

2. Combine peanut butter and 2 tablespoons butter in small saucepan; cook and stir over low heat until melted. Cool slightly.

3. Combine flour, sugar, baking powder and salt in medium bowl; mix well. Cut in ¼ cup cold butter with pastry blender or two knives until mixture resembles coarse crumbs. Stir in buttermilk just until moistened.

4. Turn out dough onto lightly floured surface; knead six to eight times. Pat dough into 8×6-inch rectangle; cut into 1-inch squares. Roll one third of squares in peanut butter mixture to coat; place in single layer in prepared pan. Top with 2 tablespoons jam, dropping jam by spoonfuls evenly over squares. Repeat layers twice.

5. Bake 35 to 40 minutes or until jam is melted and bubbly and biscuits are flaky. Cool in pan on wire rack 10 minutes. Remove biscuits from pan using foil. Serve warm.

Makes 12 servings

Cinnamon Date Scones

4 tablespoons sugar, divided

¼ teaspoon ground cinnamon

2 cups all-purpose flour

2½ teaspoons baking powder

½ teaspoon salt

5 tablespoons cold butter, cut into small pieces

½ cup chopped pitted dates

2 eggs

⅓ cup half-and-half or milk

1. Preheat oven to 425°F. Combine 2 tablespoons sugar* and cinnamon in small bowl; set aside.

2. Combine flour, remaining 2 tablespoons sugar, baking powder and salt in large bowl; mix well. Cut in butter with pastry blender or two knives until mixture resembles coarse crumbs. Stir in dates.

3. Whisk eggs and half-and-half in medium bowl until well blended. Reserve 1 tablespoon egg mixture. Add remaining egg mixture to flour mixture; stir to form soft dough that clings together and forms a ball.

4. Turn out dough onto well floured surface; knead gently 10 to 12 times. Roll out dough into 9×6-inch rectangle. Cut rectangle into six 3-inch squares; cut each square diagonally in half to make 12 triangles. Place triangles 2 inches apart on ungreased baking sheets. Brush with reserved egg mixture; sprinkle with cinnamon-sugar.

5. Bake 10 to 12 minutes or until golden brown. Remove to wire racks to cool 10 minutes. Serve warm.

*For extra sparkle and crunch, substitute 2 tablespoons sparkling or coarse sugar for the granulated sugar in the cinnamon-sugar topping mixture.

Makes 12 scones

Gingerbread Pear Muffins

1¾ cups all-purpose flour

⅓ cup sugar

2 teaspoons baking powder

¾ teaspoon ground ginger

¼ teaspoon baking soda

¼ teaspoon salt

¼ teaspoon ground cinnamon

⅓ cup milk

¼ cup vegetable oil

¼ cup light molasses

1 egg

1 medium pear, peeled and finely chopped

1. Preheat oven to 375°F. Line 12 standard (2½-inch) muffin cups with paper baking cups.

2. Sift flour, sugar, baking powder, ginger, baking soda, salt and cinnamon into large bowl.

3. Whisk milk, oil, molasses and egg in medium bowl until well blended. Stir in pear. Add to flour mixture; stir just until dry ingredients are moistened. Spoon batter evenly into prepared muffin cups.

4. Bake 20 minutes or until toothpick inserted into centers comes out clean. Remove to wire rack to cool 10 minutes. Serve warm or cool completely.

Makes 12 muffins

Parmesan Peppercorn Biscuits

2 cups all-purpose flour

⅓ cup finely grated Parmesan cheese

1 tablespoon baking powder

1 teaspoon black pepper

½ teaspoon salt

6 tablespoons (¾ stick) cold butter, cut into small pieces

1 cup buttermilk

1. Preheat oven to 425°F. Line baking sheet with parchment paper.

2. Combine flour, cheese, baking powder, pepper and salt in large bowl; mix well.

3. Cut in butter with pastry blender or two knives until mixture resembles coarse crumbs. Add buttermilk; stir just until moistened. Drop dough by ¼ cupfuls onto prepared baking sheet.

4. Bake 12 minutes or until tops of biscuits are golden brown. Remove to wire rack to cool 5 minutes. Serve warm.

Makes 12 biscuits

Carrot and Oat Muffins

- ¾ cup plus 2 tablespoons old-fashioned oats
- ¾ cup all-purpose flour
- ¾ cup whole wheat flour
- ⅓ cup sugar
- 1½ teaspoons baking powder
- 1 teaspoon ground cinnamon
- ½ teaspoon baking soda
- ¼ teaspoon salt
- ½ cup milk
- 2 eggs
- ⅓ cup unsweetened applesauce
- ¼ cup vegetable or canola oil
- ½ cup shredded carrot (1 medium to large carrot)
- ⅓ cup finely chopped walnuts (optional)

1. Preheat oven to 350°F. Spray 12 standard (2½-inch) muffin cups with nonstick cooking spray or line with paper baking cups.

2. Combine oats, all-purpose flour, whole wheat flour, sugar, baking powder, cinnamon, baking soda and salt in large bowl; mix well.

3. Whisk milk, eggs, applesauce and oil in medium bowl until blended. Stir in carrot. Add to flour mixture; stir just until dry ingredients are moistened. Spoon batter evenly into prepared muffin cups; sprinkle with walnuts, if desired.

4. Bake 20 to 22 minutes or until golden brown. Cool in pan 5 minutes; remove to wire rack to cool completely.

Makes 12 muffins

Note

These muffins are best eaten the same day.

Sweet Cherry Biscuits

2 cups all-purpose flour

¼ cup sugar

4 teaspoons baking powder

½ teaspoon salt

½ teaspoon dried rosemary (optional)

½ cup (1 stick) cold butter, cut into small pieces

¾ cup milk

½ cup dried sweetened cherries, chopped

1. Preheat oven to 425°F.

2. Combine flour, sugar, baking powder, salt and rosemary, if desired, in large bowl; mix well. Cut in butter with pastry blender or two knives until mixture forms small crumbs. Stir in milk to form sticky batter. Stir in cherries.

3. Pat dough to 1-inch thickness on floured surface. Cut out biscuits with 3-inch biscuit or cookie cutter. Place 1 inch apart on ungreased baking sheet.

4. Bake about 15 minutes or until golden brown. Remove to wire rack to cool 5 minutes. Serve warm.

Makes about 10 biscuits

Banana Walnut Muffins

2 cups all-purpose flour

2 teaspoons baking powder

½ teaspoon baking soda

½ teaspoon ground cinnamon

¼ teaspoon salt

¼ teaspoon ground nutmeg

½ cup (1 stick) butter, softened

1 cup packed brown sugar

2 eggs, lightly beaten

1 teaspoon vanilla

¼ cup sour cream

3 ripe bananas, mashed

1 cup coarsely chopped walnuts, toasted*

To toast walnuts, spread on baking sheet. Bake in preheated 350°F oven 8 to 10 minutes or until lightly browned, stirring frequently.

1. Preheat oven to 375°F. Line 12 standard (2½-inch) muffin cups with paper baking cups or spray with nonstick cooking spray.

2. Combine flour, baking powder, baking soda, cinnamon, salt and nutmeg in medium bowl; mix well.

3. Beat butter in large bowl with electric mixer at medium speed until light and fluffy. Add brown sugar; beat until well blended. Beat in eggs and vanilla until blended.

4. Stir sour cream into mashed bananas. Add to butter mixture; beat until smooth. Gradually add flour mixture; stir just until blended. Stir in walnuts. Spoon batter evenly into prepared muffin cups.

5. Bake 25 minutes or until toothpick inserted into centers comes out clean. Cool in pan 10 minutes; remove to wire rack to cool completely.

Makes 12 muffins

Cranberry Scones

2 cups all-purpose flour

¼ cup sugar

2 teaspoons baking powder

½ teaspoon salt

¼ teaspoon baking soda

½ cup (1 stick) cold butter, cut into small pieces

⅔ cup buttermilk

1 egg

½ teaspoon vanilla

½ cup chopped pecans, toasted*

½ cup dried cranberries or cherries

*To toast pecans, spread on baking sheet. Bake in preheated 350°F oven 8 to 10 minutes or until golden brown, stirring frequently.

1. Preheat oven to 350°F.

2. Combine flour, sugar, baking powder, salt and baking soda in large bowl; mix well. Cut in butter with pastry blender or two knives until mixture resembles coarse crumbs. Whisk buttermilk, egg and vanilla in small bowl until well blended. Add to flour mixture; stir just until dry ingredients are moistened. Stir in pecans and cranberries.

3. Turn out dough onto floured surface. Shape into 6-inch circle; cut into eight wedges. Place 2 inches apart on ungreased baking sheet.

4. Bake 30 to 35 minutes or until golden brown. Remove to wire rack to cool 5 minutes. Serve warm.

Makes 8 scones

Mini Corn Bread Muffins

1 cup stone ground
   cornmeal*

¾ cup all-purpose flour

2 tablespoons sugar

¾ teaspoon baking
   powder

½ teaspoon baking soda

½ teaspoon salt

1 cup buttermilk

1 egg

¼ cup vegetable or
   canola oil

*Stone ground cornmeal makes
muffins with a rustic, authentic
corn taste. It can be found
in many grocery stores and
natural food stores.*

1. Heat oven to 375°F. Spray 18 mini (1¾-inch) muffin cups with nonstick cooking spray.

2. Combine cornmeal, flour, sugar, baking powder, baking soda and salt in large bowl; mix well.

3. Whisk buttermilk, egg and oil in medium bowl until well blended. Add to flour mixture; stir just until just blended. Spoon batter evenly into prepared muffin cups.

4. Bake 13 to 15 minutes or until lightly browned and toothpick inserted into centers comes out clean. Cool in pans 5 minutes; remove to wire racks. Serve warm or at room temperature.

Makes 18 muffins

Simple Breads

Zucchini Bread

2 cups all-purpose flour

1 teaspoon salt

1 teaspoon ground cinnamon

¾ teaspoon baking powder

¾ teaspoon baking soda

¼ teaspoon ground nutmeg

½ cup vegetable oil

2 eggs

½ cup granulated sugar

½ cup packed brown sugar

1 teaspoon vanilla

2 cups packed grated zucchini (2 to 3 medium)

1. Preheat oven to 350°F. Spray 9×5-inch loaf pan with nonstick cooking spray or line with parchment paper.

2. Combine flour, salt, cinnamon, baking powder, baking soda and nutmeg in medium bowl; mix well.

3. Whisk oil, eggs, granulated sugar, brown sugar and vanilla in large bowl until well blended. Add flour mixture; stir just until dry ingredients are moistened. Stir in zucchini until blended. Pour batter into prepared pan.

4. Bake 55 to 60 minutes or until toothpick inserted into center comes out clean. Cool in pan 20 minutes; remove to wire rack to cool completely.

Makes 1 loaf

Rustic White Bread

5 cups all-purpose flour

2 cups warm water
(105° to 115°F)

1 tablespoon salt

1 package (¼ ounce)
rapid-rise or active
dry yeast

1. Combine flour and warm water in large bowl; stir to form shaggy dough. Cover with clean kitchen towel; let stand 30 minutes to hydrate flour.

2. Sprinkle salt and yeast over dough; squeeze and fold with hands to incorporate. Turn out dough onto lightly floured surface; knead 2 minutes, adding additional flour by teaspoonfuls if needed (dough will be sticky). Shape dough into a ball; return to bowl. Cover and let rise 2 hours.

3. Gently fold edges of dough to center, pressing down lightly to form a ball. Turn dough over; cover and let rise 3 to 4 hours or until dough has large air bubbles.

4. Place 5- to 6-quart Dutch oven with lid in oven; turn oven to 450°F. Preheat oven and pot 30 minutes. Meanwhile, gently ease dough from bowl onto work surface with lightly floured hands, trying not to tear as much as possible (do not punch down dough). Wrap your hands around sides of dough and gently pull it across work surface to form a ball. Repeat until dough is a smooth ball. Lightly dust medium bowl with flour; place dough in bowl. Cover and let rise while oven and pot are preheating.

5. Use oven mitts to carefully remove Dutch oven from oven and remove lid (pot and lid will be very hot). Gently turn out dough onto work surface; place in Dutch oven, bottom side up. Replace lid using oven mitts; return Dutch oven to oven.

6. Bake bread, covered, 30 minutes. Carefully remove lid; bake 10 to 12 minutes or until top is deep golden brown. Remove to wire rack to cool completely.

Makes 1 loaf

PB Banana Chocolate Chip Bread

2½ cups all-purpose flour

½ cup granulated sugar

½ cup packed brown sugar

1 tablespoon baking powder

¾ teaspoon salt

1 cup mashed ripe bananas (about 2 large)

1 cup milk

¾ cup peanut butter

¼ cup vegetable oil

1 egg, lightly beaten

1 teaspoon vanilla

1½ cups semisweet chocolate chips

1. Preheat oven to 350°F. Spray four mini (5½×3-inch) loaf pans or one 9×5-inch loaf pan with nonstick cooking spray.

2. Combine flour, granulated sugar, brown sugar, baking powder and salt in large bowl; mix well.

3. Beat bananas, milk, peanut butter, oil, egg and vanilla in medium bowl until well blended. Add banana mixture and chocolate chips to flour mixture; stir just until dry ingredients are moistened. Pour batter into prepared pans.

4. Bake 40 minutes or until toothpick inserted into centers comes out clean (65 to 75 minutes for 9×5-inch pan). Cool in pans on wire racks 10 minutes; remove to wire racks to cool completely.

Makes 4 mini loaves

Farmer-Style Sour Cream Bread

1 cup sour cream, at
   room temperature

3 tablespoons water

2½ to 3 cups all-purpose
   flour, divided

1 package (¼ ounce)
   active dry yeast

2 tablespoons sugar

1½ teaspoons salt

¼ teaspoon baking soda

1 teaspoon vegetable oil

1 tablespoon sesame
   or poppy seeds

1. Combine sour cream and water in small saucepan; heat over low heat to 110° to 120°F.

2. Combine 2 cups flour, yeast, sugar, salt and baking soda in large bowl of stand mixer. Add sour cream mixture; mix with dough hook at low speed 3 minutes. Add remaining flour, ¼ cup at a time; mix 5 minutes or until dough is smooth and elastic.

3. Line baking sheet with parchment paper. Shape dough into a ball; place on prepared baking sheet. Flatten into 8-inch circle. Brush top with oil; sprinkle with sesame seeds. Cover and let rise in warm place 1 hour or until doubled in size. Preheat oven to 350°F.

4. Bake 22 to 27 minutes or until golden brown. Remove to wire rack to cool completely.

Makes 1 loaf

Pumpkin Bread

2¼ cups all-purpose flour

1 tablespoon pumpkin pie spice

1 teaspoon baking powder

1 teaspoon baking soda

¾ teaspoon salt

3 eggs

1 can (15 ounces) pure pumpkin

1 cup granulated sugar

1 cup packed brown sugar

⅔ cup vegetable oil

1 teaspoon vanilla

¼ cup roasted salted pumpkin seeds, coarsely chopped or crushed

1. Preheat oven to 350°F. Spray two 8½×4½-inch loaf pans with nonstick cooking spray.

2. Combine flour, pumpkin pie spice, baking powder, baking soda and salt in medium bowl; mix well.

3. Whisk eggs in large bowl. Add pumpkin, granulated sugar, brown sugar, oil and vanilla; whisk until well blended. Add flour mixture; stir just until dry ingredients are moistened. Pour batter into prepared pans. Sprinkle with pumpkin seeds; pat seeds gently into batter to adhere.

4. Bake about 50 minutes or until toothpick inserted into centers comes out mostly clean with just a few moist crumbs. Cool in pans 10 minutes; remove to wire racks to cool completely.

Makes 2 loaves

Note

The recipe can be made in one 9×5-inch loaf pan instead of two 8½×4½-inch pans. Bake about 1 hour 20 minutes or until toothpick inserted into center comes out with just a few moist crumbs. Check bread after 50 minutes; cover loosely with foil if top is browning too quickly.

Quattro Formaggio Focaccia

1 tablespoon sugar

1 package (¼ ounce) instant yeast

1¼ cups warm water (100° to 105°F)

3 to 3¼ cups all-purpose flour

¼ cup plus 2 tablespoons olive oil, divided

1 teaspoon salt

¼ cup marinara sauce with basil

1 cup (4 ounces) shredded Italian cheese blend

1. Dissolve sugar and yeast in warm water in large bowl of stand mixer; let stand 5 minutes or until bubbly. Stir in 3 cups flour, ¼ cup oil and salt with spoon or spatula to form rough dough. Mix with dough hook at low speed 5 minutes, adding additional flour, 1 tablespoon at a time, if necessary for dough to come together. (Dough will be sticky and will not clean side of bowl.)

2. Shape dough into a ball. Place dough in large greased bowl; turn to grease top. Cover and let rise 1 to 1½ hours or until doubled in size.

3. Punch down dough. Pour remaining 2 tablespoons oil into 13×9-inch baking pan; pat and stretch dough to fill pan. Make indentations in top of dough with fingertips.

4. Spread marinara sauce evenly over dough; sprinkle with cheese. Cover and let rise 30 minutes or until puffy. Preheat oven to 425°F.

5. Bake 17 to 20 minutes or until golden brown. Cut into squares or strips.

Makes 12 servings

Blueberry Hill Bread

2 cups all-purpose flour

¾ cup packed brown sugar

2 teaspoons baking powder

1 teaspoon baking soda

1 teaspoon salt

½ teaspoon ground nutmeg

¾ cup buttermilk

1 egg

¼ cup vegetable oil or melted butter

1 cup fresh or thawed frozen blueberries

1. Preheat oven to 350°F. Spray 8½×4½-inch loaf pan with nonstick cooking spray.

2. Combine flour, brown sugar, baking powder, baking soda, salt and nutmeg in food processor; process 5 seconds to mix. Whisk buttermilk, egg and oil in medium bowl until blended. Pour over flour mixture; process 5 to 10 seconds or just until dry ingredients are moistened. *Do not overprocess.* Batter should be lumpy.

3. Sprinkle blueberries over batter; pulse several times just to incorporate blueberries into batter. (Batter will be stiff.) Pour batter into prepared pan.

4. Bake 50 to 60 minutes or until toothpick inserted into center comes out clean. Cool in pan 15 minutes; remove to wire rack to cool completely.

Makes 1 loaf

Walnut Fig Bread

1 cup honey beer or water

2 tablespoons butter or olive oil

1 tablespoon honey

2¼ cups all-purpose flour, divided

1 cup whole wheat flour

1 package (¼ ounce) active dry yeast

1 tablespoon whole fennel seeds

1½ teaspoons salt

1 egg, beaten

1 cup chopped dried figs or dates

½ cup chopped walnuts, toasted*

*To toast walnuts, cook in medium skillet over medium heat 2 minutes or until lightly browned, stirring frequently.

1. Combine beer, butter and honey in small saucepan; heat over low heat to 120°F.

2. Combine 1 cup all-purpose flour, whole wheat flour, yeast, fennel seeds and salt in large bowl of stand mixer. Add beer mixture; beat with paddle attachment at medium-low speed 3 minutes. Add egg; beat until blended.

3. Replace paddle attachment with dough hook. Add remaining all-purpose flour, ¼ cup at a time; mix at low speed to form soft dough. Add figs and walnuts; mix about 5 minutes or until dough is smooth and elastic.

4. Shape dough into a ball. Place dough in greased bowl; turn to grease top. Cover and let rise in warm place about 1 hour or until doubled in size.

5. Line baking sheet with parchment paper. Punch down dough. Shape dough into round loaf; place on prepared baking sheet. Cover and let rise in warm place 40 minutes or until doubled in size. Preheat oven to 350°F.

6. Bake 30 to 35 minutes or until golden brown and bread sounds hollow when tapped. Remove to wire rack to cool completely.

Makes 1 loaf

Pesto Rolls

3 cups all-purpose flour, divided

1 package (¼ ounce) rapid-rise yeast

1½ teaspoons salt

1 cup warm water (120°F)

2 tablespoons olive oil

½ cup refrigerated pesto sauce

1 cup (4 ounces) shredded mozzarella cheese

⅓ cup grated Parmesan cheese

¼ cup chopped drained oil-packed sun-dried tomatoes

1. Combine 1½ cups flour, yeast and salt in large bowl of stand mixer; mix with paddle attachment at low speed to blend. Add warm water and oil; beat at medium speed 2 minutes.

2. Replace paddle attachment with dough hook. Add remaining 1½ cups flour; mix at low speed 5 to 7 minutes or until dough is smooth and elastic. Shape dough into a ball. Place dough in greased bowl; turn to grease top. Cover and let rise in warm place about 45 minutes or until doubled in size.

3. Spray 12×8-inch baking pan with nonstick cooking spray. Turn out dough onto lightly floured surface; roll into 18×12-inch rectangle. Spread pesto evenly over dough; sprinkle with mozzarella, Parmesan and sun-dried tomatoes. Starting with long side, roll up dough jelly-roll style; pinch seam to seal. Trim ends; cut roll crosswise into 12 (1½-inch) slices.

4. Place slices cut sides up in prepared pan; cover and let rise in warm place about 30 minutes or until rolls are puffy and almost doubled in size. Preheat oven to 350°F.

5. Bake 22 to 27 minutes or until lightly browned. Cool slightly before serving.

Makes 12 rolls

Loaded Banana Bread

1½ cups all-purpose flour

2½ teaspoons baking powder

¼ teaspoon salt

6 tablespoons (¾ stick) butter, softened

⅓ cup granulated sugar

⅓ cup packed brown sugar

2 eggs

3 ripe bananas, mashed

½ teaspoon vanilla

1 can (8 ounces) crushed pineapple, drained

⅓ cup flaked coconut

¼ cup mini chocolate chips

⅓ cup chopped walnuts (optional)

1. Preheat oven to 350°F. Spray 9×5-inch loaf pan with nonstick cooking spray.

2. Combine flour, baking powder and salt in small bowl; mix well.

3. Beat butter, granulated sugar and brown sugar in large bowl with electric mixer at medium speed until light and fluffy. Beat in eggs, one at a time, scraping down bowl after each addition. Add bananas and vanilla; beat until blended.

4. Gradually add flour mixture; beat just until combined. Fold in pineapple, coconut and chocolate chips until blended. Spread batter in prepared pan; sprinkle with walnuts, if desired.

5. Bake 50 minutes or until toothpick inserted into center comes out almost clean. Cool in pan 1 hour; remove to wire rack to cool completely.

Makes 1 loaf

Red Pepper Bread

2 to 2½ cups all-purpose flour, divided

1 cup whole wheat flour

2 tablespoons grated Parmesan cheese

1 teaspoon dried rosemary, plus additional for topping

1 package (¼ ounce) rapid-rise yeast

½ teaspoon salt

¼ teaspoon dried thyme

1¼ cups hot water (130°F)

1 tablespoon olive or vegetable oil

½ cup chopped roasted red pepper

1 egg white, beaten

2 teaspoons water

1. Combine 1 cup all-purpose flour, whole wheat flour, cheese, 1 teaspoon rosemary, yeast, salt and thyme in large bowl; mix well. Stir in hot water and oil until blended. Stir in roasted pepper. Stir in enough remaining all-purpose flour to form soft dough.

2. Turn out dough onto lightly floured surface; flatten slightly. Knead gently 2 to 3 minutes or until smooth and elastic, adding additional all-purpose flour to prevent sticking, if necessary. Place dough in large greased bowl; turn to grease top. Cover and let rise in warm place 30 minutes or until doubled in size.

3. Line baking sheet with parchment paper. Punch down dough. Shape dough into one large or two small round loaves on prepared baking sheet. Cover and let rise 30 minutes or until doubled in size.

4. Preheat oven to 375°F. Slash top of dough with sharp knife. Whisk egg white and 2 teaspoons water in small cup; brush over dough. Sprinkle with additional rosemary, if desired.

5. Bake 35 to 40 minutes for one large loaf, 25 to 30 minutes for two small loaves or until bread is golden brown and sounds hollow when gently tapped. Cool completely on wire rack.

Makes 1 large loaf or 2 small loaves

Boston Black Coffee Bread

½ cup rye flour

½ cup cornmeal

½ cup whole wheat flour

1 teaspoon baking soda

½ teaspoon salt

¾ cup strong brewed coffee, room temperature or cold

⅓ cup molasses

¼ cup canola oil

¾ cup raisins

1. Preheat oven to 325°F. Grease and flour 9×5-inch loaf pan.

2. Combine rye flour, cornmeal, whole wheat flour, baking soda and salt in medium bowl; mix well. Add coffee, molasses and oil; stir just until mixture forms thick batter. Fold in raisins. Spread batter in prepared pan.

3. Bake 50 minutes or until toothpick inserted into center comes out clean. Cool completely in pan on wire rack.

Makes 1 loaf

Tip

To cool hot coffee, pour it over 2 ice cubes in a measuring cup to measure ¾ cup total. Let stand 10 minutes to cool.

Cranberry Brie Bubble Bread

3 cups all-purpose flour

1 package (¼ ounce) rapid-rise yeast

1 teaspoon salt

1 cup warm water (120°F)

¼ cup plus 2 tablespoons butter, melted, divided

¾ cup finely chopped pecans or walnuts

¼ cup packed brown sugar

¼ teaspoon coarse salt

1 package (7 ounces) Brie cheese, cut into ¼-inch pieces

1 cup whole-berry cranberry sauce

1. Combine flour, yeast and 1 teaspoon salt in large bowl of stand mixer. Stir in warm water and 2 tablespoons melted butter to form rough dough. Mix with dough hook at low speed 5 to 7 minutes or until dough is smooth and elastic.

2. Shape dough into a ball. Place in greased bowl; turn to grease top. Cover and let rise in warm place about 45 minutes or until doubled in size.

3. Spray 2-quart baking dish or ovenproof bowl with nonstick cooking spray. Combine pecans, brown sugar and coarse salt in shallow bowl; mix well. Place remaining ¼ cup butter in another shallow bowl. Turn out dough onto lightly floured surface; pat and stretch into 9×6-inch rectangle. Cut dough into 1-inch pieces; roll into balls.

4. Dip balls of dough in butter; roll in pecan mixture to coat. Place in prepared baking dish, layering with cheese and spoonfuls of cranberry sauce. Cover and let rise in warm place about 45 minutes or until dough is puffy. Preheat oven to 350°F.

5. Bake 30 minutes or until dough is firm and filling is bubbly. Cool on wire rack 15 to 20 minutes. Serve warm.

Makes 12 servings

Brown Soda Bread

2 cups all-purpose flour

1 cup whole wheat flour

1 teaspoon baking soda

½ teaspoon salt

½ teaspoon ground ginger

1¼ to 1½ cups buttermilk

3 tablespoons dark molasses (preferably blackstrap)

1. Preheat oven to 375°F. Line baking sheet with parchment paper.

2. Combine 2 cups all-purpose flour, whole wheat flour, baking soda, salt and ginger in large bowl; mix well. Combine 1¼ cups buttermilk and molasses in medium bowl; mix well. Stir into flour mixture. Add additional buttermilk, 1 tablespoon at a time, if necessary to make dry, rough dough.

3. Turn out dough onto floured surface; knead 8 to 10 times or just until smooth. *Do not overknead.* Shape dough into round loaf about 1½ inches thick. Place on prepared baking sheet.

4. Use floured knife to cut halfway through dough, scoring into quarters. Sprinkle top of dough with additional all-purpose flour, if desired.

5. Bake about 35 minutes or until bread sounds hollow when tapped. Remove to wire rack to cool slightly. Serve warm.

Makes 1 loaf

Focaccia with Onion and Thyme

3 to 3¼ cups bread flour, divided

1 package (¼ ounce) active dry yeast

1 tablespoon sugar

1 teaspoon salt

1 cup warm water (120°F)

2 tablespoons olive oil, divided

1 small red onion, cut in half and thinly sliced

6 to 8 sprigs fresh thyme *or* 1 teaspoon dried thyme

¼ cup grated Parmesan cheese

1. Combine 1 cup flour, yeast, sugar and salt in large bowl of stand mixer. Add warm water and 1 tablespoon oil; beat with paddle attachment at medium speed 4 minutes. Replace paddle attachment with dough hook. Gradually add 2 cups flour; mix at low speed 5 minutes or until dough is smooth and elastic, adding remaining flour, 1 tablespoon at at time, if necessary to prevent sticking.

2. Shape dough into a ball. Place dough in large greased bowl; turn to grease top. Cover and let rise in warm place about 1 hour or until doubled in size.

3. Meanwhile, heat ½ tablespoon oil in medium skillet over medium heat. Add onion; cook and stir 5 minutes or until softened. Set aside to cool.

4. Line baking sheet with parchment paper. Punch down dough. Turn out dough onto lightly floured surface; roll or press into 12-inch circle. Place on prepared baking sheet; cover and let rise 30 minutes.

5. Preheat oven to 375°F. Brush dough with remaining ½ tablespoon oil; top with sautéed onion, thyme and cheese.

6. Bake about 25 minutes or until golden brown. Remove to wire rack to cool.

Makes about 8 servings

Applesauce Spice Bread

1½ cups all-purpose flour

1 cup unsweetened applesauce

¾ cup packed brown sugar

¼ cup (½ stick) butter, softened

1 egg

1 teaspoon vanilla

¾ teaspoon baking soda

¾ teaspoon ground cinnamon

¼ teaspoon baking powder

¼ teaspoon salt

¼ teaspoon ground nutmeg

½ cup chopped walnuts, toasted*

½ cup raisins (optional)

Powdered sugar

To toast walnuts, spread on baking sheet. Bake in preheated 350°F oven 6 to 8 minutes or until lightly browned, stirring frequently.

1. Preheat oven to 350°F. Spray 9-inch square baking pan with nonstick cooking spray.

2. Combine flour, applesauce, brown sugar, butter, egg, vanilla, baking soda, cinnamon, baking powder, salt and nutmeg in large bowl; beat with electric mixer at low speed 30 seconds. Beat at high speed 3 minutes. Stir in walnuts and raisins, if desired. Pour batter into prepared pan.

3. Bake 30 minutes or until toothpick inserted into center comes out clean. Cool completely in pan on wire rack. Sprinkle with powdered sugar just before serving.

Makes 9 servings

Foolproof Cookies

Chocolate Hazelnut Sandwich Cookies

¾ cup (1½ sticks) butter, slightly softened

¾ cup sugar

3 egg yolks

1 teaspoon vanilla

2 cups all-purpose flour

¼ teaspoon salt

⅔ cup chocolate hazelnut spread

1. Beat butter and sugar in large bowl with electric mixer at medium speed 1 minute. Beat in egg yolks and vanilla until well blended. Add flour and salt; beat at low speed just until combined. Divide dough in half. Shape each piece into 6×1½-inch log. Wrap in plastic wrap; refrigerate at least 2 hours or until firm.

2. Preheat oven to 350°F. Line cookie sheets with parchment paper. Cut dough into ⅛-inch-thick slices; place 1 inch apart on prepared cookie sheets.

3. Bake 10 to 12 minutes or until edges are lightly browned. Cool on cookie sheets 5 minutes; remove to wire racks to cool completely.

4. Spread 1 teaspoon chocolate hazelnut spread on flat side of half of cookies; top with remaining cookies.

Makes 30 sandwich cookies

Note
The dough can be refrigerated up to 3 days or may be frozen for up to 1 month.

Mocha Madness

1 cup all-purpose flour

½ teaspoon salt

½ teaspoon baking soda

½ cup (1 stick) butter, softened

½ cup packed brown sugar

¼ cup granulated sugar

1 egg

1 teaspoon vanilla

½ cup chopped pecans

1 bar (3 ounces) coffee-flavored chocolate, finely chopped

Latte Glaze (recipe follows)

1. Preheat oven to 350°F. Line cookie sheets with parchment paper or lightly grease. Combine flour, salt and baking soda in small bowl; mix well.

2. Beat butter, brown sugar and granulated sugar in large bowl with electric mixer at medium speed until creamy. Add egg and vanilla; beat until well blended, scraping down side of bowl once. Gradually add flour mixture, beating at low speed until blended. Stir in pecans and chocolate.

3. Drop dough by tablespoonfuls 3 inches apart onto prepared cookie sheets.

4. Bake 10 to 12 minutes or until set and lightly browned. Cool on cookie sheets 5 minutes; remove to wire racks to cool completely.

5. Prepare Latte Glaze; drizzle over cookies. Let stand 30 minutes or until set.

Makes 3 dozen cookies

Latte Glaze

Combine 1 teaspoon instant coffee granules, 1 tablespoon half-and-half and ⅛ teaspoon salt in small microwavable bowl; microwave on HIGH 15 seconds or until coffee dissolves. Stir in ½ cup powdered sugar until smooth. Stir in additional half-and-half, 1 teaspoon at a time, if necessary to reach desired consistency.

Lemon Drops

2 cups all-purpose flour

⅛ teaspoon salt

1 cup (2 sticks) butter, softened

1 cup powdered sugar, divided

Grated peel of 1 lemon

2 teaspoons lemon juice

1. Preheat oven to 300°F. Combine flour and salt in medium bowl; mix well.

2. Beat butter and ¾ cup powdered sugar in large bowl with electric mixer at medium speed until fluffy. Beat in lemon peel and juice until well blended. Add flour mixture, ½ cup at a time; beat at low speed just until blended after each addition.

3. Shape dough by rounded teaspoonfuls into balls. Place 1 inch apart on ungreased cookie sheets.

4. Bake 20 to 25 minutes or until bottoms are lightly browned. Cool on cookie sheets 5 minutes; remove to wire racks to cool completely. Sprinkle with remaining ¼ cup powdered sugar.

Makes about 6 dozen cookies

Chunky Double Chocolate Cookies

2 cups all-purpose flour

1½ teaspoons baking powder

½ teaspoon salt

1½ cups packed brown sugar

¾ cup (1½ sticks) butter, softened

1 teaspoon vanilla

2 eggs

4 ounces unsweetened chocolate, melted

12 ounces white chocolate, chopped *or* 1 package (12 ounces) white chocolate chips

1 cup chopped nuts (optional)

1. Preheat oven to 350°F. Combine flour, baking powder and salt in medium bowl; mix well.

2. Beat brown sugar, butter and vanilla in large bowl with electric mixer at medium speed about 3 minutes or until light and fluffy. Add eggs; beat until well blended. Beat in melted chocolate until blended. Gradually add flour mixture, beating at low speed until blended. Stir in white chocolate and nuts, if desired.

3. Drop dough by rounded tablespoonfuls 2 inches apart onto ungreased cookie sheets.

4. Bake 11 to 12 minutes or until set. Cool on cookie sheets 1 minute; remove to wire racks to cool completely.

Makes about 3½ dozen cookies

Flourless Peanut Butter Cookies

1 cup packed brown sugar

1 cup creamy peanut butter

1 egg, lightly beaten

½ cup semisweet chocolate chips, melted

1. Preheat oven to 350°F. Beat brown sugar, peanut butter and egg in medium bowl until blended and smooth.

2. Shape dough into 24 (1½-inch) balls. Place 2 inches apart on ungreased cookie sheets. Flatten dough slightly with fork.

3. Bake 10 to 12 minutes or until set. Remove to wire racks to cool completely.

4. Drizzle melted chocolate over cookies; let stand until set.

Makes 2 dozen cookies

Variation

Press a milk chocolate star or kiss into each ball of dough before baking instead of drizzling with melted chocolate.

Pistachio Crescent Cookies

2 cups all-purpose flour

2 cups finely chopped salted pistachio nuts, divided

¼ teaspoon salt

1¼ cups (2½ sticks) butter, softened, divided

¾ cup powdered sugar

½ cup mini chocolate chips

⅔ cup semisweet chocolate chips

1. Line cookie sheets with parchment paper. Combine flour, 1½ cups pistachios and salt in medium bowl; mix well.

2. Beat 1 cup butter and powdered sugar in large bowl with electric mixer at medium speed about 3 minutes or until light and fluffy. Gradually add flour mixture, beating at low speed just until blended. Stir in mini chocolate chips.

3. Roll 1½ teaspoons dough into 2½-inch ropes; bend into crescent shapes. Arrange 1 inch apart on prepared cookie sheets. Refrigerate 30 minutes. Preheat oven to 300°F.

4. Bake cookies 10 minutes or until firm and lightly browned. Cool on cookie sheets 1 minute; remove to wire racks to cool completely.

5. For glaze, combine ⅔ cup chocolate chips and remaining ¼ cup butter in medium microwavable bowl; microwave on LOW (30%) 1 minute. Stir and repeat if necessary until chocolate is melted and mixture is smooth.

6. Place cookies on wire racks set over waxed paper. Place remaining ½ cup pistachios in small bowl. Dip one end of each cookie in chocolate, then in nuts. Let stand 30 minutes or until glaze is set.

Makes about 6 dozen cookies

Snickerdoodles

¾ cup plus 2 tablespoons sugar, divided

2 teaspoons ground cinnamon, divided

1⅓ cups all-purpose flour

1 teaspoon cream of tartar

½ teaspoon baking soda

½ teaspoon salt

½ cup (1 stick) butter, softened

1 egg

1. Preheat oven to 375°F. Line cookie sheets with parchment paper. Combine 2 tablespoons sugar and 1 teaspoon cinnamon in small bowl.

2. Combine flour, remaining 1 teaspoon cinnamon, cream of tartar, baking soda and salt in medium bowl; mix well. Beat remaining ¾ cup sugar and butter in large bowl with electric mixer at medium speed until creamy. Beat in egg until blended. Gradually add flour mixture, beating at low speed until stiff dough forms.

3. Roll dough into 1-inch balls; roll in cinnamon-sugar to coat. Place on prepared cookie sheets.

4. Bake 10 minutes or until cookies are set. *Do not overbake.* Remove to wire racks to cool completely.

Makes about 3 dozen cookies

Chocolate Coconut Toffee Delights

½ cup all-purpose flour

¼ teaspoon baking powder

¼ teaspoon salt

1 package (12 ounces) semisweet chocolate chips, divided

¼ cup (½ stick) butter, cut into small pieces

¾ cup packed brown sugar

2 eggs

1 teaspoon vanilla

1½ cups flaked coconut

1 cup toffee baking bits

½ cup bittersweet chocolate chips, melted

1. Preheat oven to 350°F. Line cookie sheets with parchment paper. Combine flour, baking powder and salt in small bowl; mix well.

2. Combine 1 cup semisweet chocolate chips and butter in medium microwavable bowl; microwave on HIGH 1 minute. Stir; microwave at additional 30-second intervals until mixture is melted and smooth, stirring after each interval.

3. Beat brown sugar, eggs and vanilla in large bowl with electric mixer at medium speed about 2 minutes or until creamy. Add chocolate mixture; beat until well blended. Gradually add flour mixture, beating at low speed just until blended. Stir in coconut, toffee bits and remaining 1 cup semisweet chocolate chips.

4. Drop dough by heaping ⅓ cupfuls 3 inches apart onto prepared cookie sheets. Flatten into 3½-inch circles with spatula.

5. Bake 15 to 17 minutes or until edges are firm to the touch. Cool on cookie sheets 2 minutes; slide parchment paper and cookies onto wire racks to cool completely.

6. Drizzle melted bittersweet chocolate over cookies; let stand until set.

Makes 1 dozen large cookies

Orange Almond Sables

¾ cup whole blanched almonds, toasted*

1¾ cups all-purpose flour

¼ teaspoon salt

1½ cups powdered sugar

1 cup (2 sticks) butter, softened

1 tablespoon finely grated orange peel

1 tablespoon almond-flavored liqueur *or* 1 teaspoon almond extract

1 egg, beaten

To toast almonds, spread on baking sheet. Bake in preheated 350°F oven 8 to 10 minutes or until golden brown, stirring frequently.

1. Preheat oven to 375°F. Reserve 24 whole almonds; set aside. Place remaining cooled almonds in food processor; pulse until almonds are ground but not pasty.

2. Combine ground almonds, flour and salt in medium bowl; mix well. Beat powdered sugar and butter in large bowl with electric mixer at medium speed about 3 minutes or until light and fluffy. Beat in orange peel and liqueur. Gradually add flour mixture, beating at low speed until well blended.

3. Roll out dough to ¼-inch thickness on lightly floured surface with lightly floured rolling pin. Cut out dough with floured 2½-inch round cookie cutter. Place cutouts 2 inches apart on ungreased cookie sheets.

4. Lightly brush tops of cutouts with beaten egg. Press one reserved whole almond in center of each cutout; brush almonds lightly with beaten egg.

5. Bake 10 to 12 minutes or until light golden brown. Cool on cookie sheets 1 minute; remove to wire racks to cool completely.

Makes about 2 dozen cookies

Chocolate-Dipped Cinnamon Thins

1¼ cups all-purpose flour

1½ teaspoons ground cinnamon

¼ teaspoon salt

1 cup (2 sticks) butter, softened

1 cup powdered sugar

1 egg

1 teaspoon vanilla

4 ounces chopped bittersweet chocolate, melted

1. Combine flour, cinnamon and salt in small bowl; mix well. Beat butter in large bowl with electric mixer at medium speed about 2 minutes or until creamy. Add powdered sugar; beat until well blended. Beat in egg and vanilla. Gradually add flour mixture, beating at low speed just until blended.

2. Place dough on sheet of waxed paper. Using waxed paper to hold dough, roll back and forth to form log about 2½ inches in diameter and 12 inches long. Wrap tightly in plastic wrap; refrigerate at least 2 hours or until firm. (Dough may be frozen up to 3 months; thaw in refrigerator before baking.)

3. Preheat oven to 350°F. Cut dough into ¼-inch-thick slices. Place 2 inches apart on ungreased cookie sheets.

4. Bake 10 minutes or until set. Cool on cookie sheets 2 minutes; remove to wire racks to cool completely.

5. Dip half of each cookie into melted chocolate. Place on waxed paper; let stand about 40 minutes or until chocolate is set.

Makes about 2 dozen cookies

Little Oatmeal Cookies

¾ **cup all-purpose flour**

½ **teaspoon baking soda**

½ **teaspoon ground cinnamon**

¼ **teaspoon salt**

½ **cup (1 stick) butter, softened**

½ **cup packed brown sugar**

¼ **cup granulated sugar**

1 **egg**

1 **teaspoon vanilla**

1½ **cups quick or old-fashioned oats**

½ **cup raisins**

1. Preheat oven to 350°F. Combine flour, baking soda, cinnamon and salt in small bowl; mix well.

2. Beat butter, brown sugar and granulated sugar in large bowl with electric mixer at medium speed about 2 minutes or until creamy. Add egg and vanilla; beat until well blended. Gradually add flour mixture, beating at low speed until blended. Stir in oats and raisins.

3. Drop dough by scant teaspoonfuls 2 inches apart onto ungreased cookie sheets.

4. Bake 7 minutes or just until edges are lightly browned. Cool on cookie sheets 1 minute; remove to wire racks to cool completely.

Makes about 6 dozen cookies

Pumpkin White Chocolate Drops

1 cup granulated sugar

1 cup (2 sticks) butter, softened

½ (15-ounce) can pure pumpkin

1 egg

2 cups all-purpose flour

1 teaspoon pumpkin pie spice*

½ teaspoon baking powder

¼ teaspoon baking soda

1 cup white chocolate chips

1 cup prepared cream cheese frosting

*Or substitute ½ teaspoon ground cinnamon, ¼ teaspoon ground ginger, ⅛ teaspoon ground allspice and ⅛ teaspoon ground nutmeg.

1. Preheat oven to 375°F. Line cookie sheets with parchment paper or spray with nonstick cooking spray.

2. Beat granulated sugar and butter in large bowl with electric mixer at medium speed about 3 minutes or until light and fluffy. Add pumpkin and egg; beat until well blended. Add flour, pumpkin pie spice, baking powder and baking soda; beat at low speed just until blended. Stir in white chocolate chips.

3. Drop dough by tablespoonfuls about 2 inches apart onto prepared cookie sheets.

4. Bake 16 minutes or until set and lightly browned. Cool on cookie sheets 1 minute; remove to wire racks to cool completely.

5. Spread frosting over cookies.

Makes about 3 dozen cookies

Rosemary Honey Shortbread Cookies

2 cups all-purpose flour

1 tablespoon fresh rosemary leaves,* minced

½ teaspoon salt

½ teaspoon baking powder

¾ cup (1½ sticks) unsalted butter, softened

½ cup powdered sugar

2 tablespoons honey

*For best flavor, use only fresh rosemary or substitute fresh or dried lavender buds.

1. Combine flour, rosemary, salt and baking powder in medium bowl; mix well.

2. Beat butter, powdered sugar and honey in large bowl with electric mixer at medium speed until creamy. Gradually add flour mixture, beating at low speed just until blended. (Dough will be crumbly.)

3. Shape dough into log. Wrap in plastic wrap; refrigerate 1 hour or until firm. (Dough can be refrigerated several days before baking.)

4. Preheat oven to 350°F. Line cookie sheets with parchment paper. Cut dough into ½-inch slices; place 2 inches apart on prepared cookie sheets.

5. Bake 13 minutes or until set. Cool on cookie sheets 1 minute; remove to wire racks to cool completely.

Makes 2 dozen cookies

Tiny Peanut Butter Sandwiches

1¼ cups all-purpose flour

½ teaspoon baking powder

½ teaspoon baking soda

¼ teaspoon salt

½ cup (1 stick) butter, softened

½ cup granulated sugar

½ cup packed brown sugar

½ cup creamy peanut butter

1 egg

1 teaspoon vanilla

1 cup semisweet chocolate chips

½ cup whipping cream

1. Preheat oven to 350°F. Combine flour, baking powder, baking soda and salt in medium bowl; mix well.

2. Beat butter, granulated sugar and brown sugar in large bowl with electric mixer at medium speed about 3 minutes or until light and fluffy. Beat in peanut butter, egg and vanilla until well blended. Gradually add flour mixture, beating at low speed until blended.

3. Shape dough by ½ teaspoonfuls into balls; place 1 inch apart on ungreased cookie sheets. Use fork to flatten balls slightly and press criss-cross pattern into dough.

4. Bake 6 minutes or just until set. Cool on cookie sheets 4 minutes; remove to wire racks to cool completely.

5. For filling, place chocolate chips in medium bowl. Place cream in small microwavable bowl; microwave on HIGH 2 minutes or just until simmering. Pour cream over chocolate chips; let stand 2 minutes. Stir until smooth; let stand 10 minutes or until filling thickens to desired consistency.

6. Spread scant teaspoon filling on flat side of half of cookies; top with remaining cookies.

Makes 6 to 7 dozen sandwich cookies

Double Chocolate Brownie Cookies

1⅔ cups all-purpose flour

½ teaspoon baking soda

½ teaspoon salt

1 package (about 11 ounces) semisweet or dark chocolate chips, divided

½ cup (1 stick) butter, softened

½ cup packed brown sugar

¼ cup granulated sugar

2 eggs

¾ teaspoon vanilla

¾ cup chopped walnuts (optional)

1. Preheat oven to 350°F. Line cookie sheets with parchment paper. Combine flour, baking soda and salt in medium bowl; mix well.

2. Place ¾ cup chocolate chips in small microwavable bowl; microwave on LOW (30% power) 2 minutes. Stir; microwave 1 minute or until chocolate is melted.

3. Beat butter, brown sugar and granulated sugar in large bowl with electric mixer at medium speed about 3 minutes or until light and creamy. Add eggs, one at a time, beating well and scraping down side of bowl after each addition. Beat in vanilla. Add melted chocolate; beat until well blended. Gradually add flour mixture, beating at low speed just until blended. Stir in remaining chocolate chips and walnuts, if desired.

4. Drop dough by tablespoonfuls onto prepared cookie sheets.

5. Bake 8 minutes or just until edges of cookies are set but centers are still soft. Cool on cookie sheets 2 minutes; remove to wire racks to cool completely.

Makes 3 dozen cookies

Ginger Molasses Spice Cookies

2 cups all-purpose flour

1½ teaspoons ground ginger

1 teaspoon baking soda

½ teaspoon salt

½ teaspoon ground cinnamon

½ teaspoon ground cloves

1¼ cups sugar, divided

¾ cup (1½ sticks) butter, softened

¼ cup molasses

1 egg

1. Preheat oven to 375°F. Combine flour, ginger, baking soda, salt, cinnamon and cloves in medium bowl; mix well.

2. Beat 1 cup sugar and butter in large bowl with electric mixer at medium speed about 3 minutes or until light and fluffy. Add molasses and egg; beat until well blended. Gradually add flour mixture, beating at low speed just until blended.

3. Place remaining ¼ cup sugar in shallow bowl. Shape dough by ½ teaspoonfuls into balls; roll in sugar to coat. Place 1 inch apart on ungreased cookie sheets.

4. Bake 7 to 8 minutes or until almost set. Cool on cookie sheets 2 minutes; remove to wire racks to cool completely.

Makes about 12 dozen cookies

Brownies & Bars

Chocolate Chip Shortbread

½ cup (1 stick) butter, softened

½ cup granulated sugar

2 tablespoons packed brown sugar

1 teaspoon vanilla

1 cup all-purpose flour

½ teaspoon salt

½ cup plus 2 tablespoons mini semisweet chocolate chips, divided

1. Preheat oven to 350°F.

2. Beat butter, granulated sugar and brown sugar in large bowl with electric mixer at medium speed about 3 minutes or until light and fluffy. Beat in vanilla. Add flour and salt; beat at low speed just until combined. Stir in ½ cup chocolate chips.

3. Press dough into 8- or 9-inch square baking pan. Sprinkle with remaining 2 tablespoons chocolate chips; press lightly into dough.

4. Bake 15 to 17 minutes or until edges are golden brown. Cool completely in pan on wire rack. Cut into rectangles.

Makes 12 to 16 bars

Frosted Cocoa Brownies

2 cups all-purpose flour

2 cups granulated sugar

½ teaspoon salt

½ cup buttermilk

2 eggs, lightly beaten

1 teaspoon baking soda

1 teaspoon vanilla

1 cup (2 sticks) butter

1 cup hot coffee

¼ cup unsweetened
   cocoa powder

Cocoa Frosting
   (recipe follows)

1. Preheat oven to 400°F. Spray 17½×11-inch jelly-roll pan with nonstick cooking spray.

2. Combine flour, granulated sugar and salt in large bowl; mix well. Whisk buttermilk, eggs, baking soda and vanilla in small bowl until blended.

3. Combine butter, coffee and cocoa in medium saucepan; bring to a simmer over medium heat, stirring frequently until butter is melted and mixture is smooth. Add to flour mixture; stir until blended. Stir in buttermilk mixture until well blended. Pour batter into prepared pan.

4. Bake 20 minutes or until center springs back when touched. Meanwhile, prepare Cocoa Frosting.

5. Remove brownies from oven; immediately pour warm frosting over hot brownies, spreading evenly. Cool in pan on wire rack.

Makes 3 dozen brownies

Cocoa Frosting

Combine ½ cup (1 stick) butter, 2 tablespoons unsweetened cocoa powder and ¼ cup milk in large saucepan; bring to a boil over medium heat. Remove from heat; stir in 3½ cups powdered sugar and 1 teaspoon vanilla until smooth.

Southern Caramel Apple Bars

2 cups all-purpose flour

1 teaspoon salt

½ teaspoon baking powder

½ teaspoon baking soda

⅔ cup butter

¾ cup packed brown sugar

½ cup granulated sugar

1 egg

1 teaspoon vanilla

4 Granny Smith apples, peeled and coarsely chopped

½ cup pecans, chopped

24 caramel candies, unwrapped

2 tablespoons milk

1. Preheat oven to 350°F. Spray 13×9-inch baking pan with nonstick cooking spray.

2. Combine flour, salt, baking powder and baking soda in medium bowl; mix well. Melt butter in medium saucepan over medium heat. Remove from heat; stir in brown sugar and granulated sugar. Add egg and vanilla; stir until well blended. Add flour mixture; stir until blended. Press into bottom of prepared pan; top with apples.

3. Bake 40 to 45 minutes or until edges are browned and pulling away from sides of pan. Cool completely in pan on wire rack.

4. Toast pecans in medium nonstick skillet over medium-high heat 2 minutes or until fragrant, stirring frequently. Remove to small bowl; set aside. Wipe out skillet with paper towel. Add caramels and milk to skillet; heat over medium-low heat until melted and smooth, stirring constantly.

5. Drizzle caramel sauce over cooled apple bars; sprinkle with pecans. Let stand 30 minutes before cutting.

Makes 2 to 3 dozen bars

Toffee Latte Nut Bars

1½ cups all-purpose flour

¼ cup powdered sugar

½ teaspoon salt

¾ cup (1½ sticks) cold butter, cut into small pieces

2 teaspoons instant coffee granules

1 teaspoon hot water

1 can (14 ounces) sweetened condensed milk

1 egg

1 teaspoon vanilla

1 package (8 ounces) toffee baking bits

1 cup chopped walnuts or pecans

¾ cup flaked coconut *or* 1 cup large coconut flakes

1. Preheat oven to 350°F. Line 13×9-inch pan with parchment paper or spray with nonstick cooking spray.

2. Combine flour, powdered sugar and salt in large bowl; mix well. Cut in butter with pastry blender or electric mixer at low speed until mixture resembles coarse crumbs. Press into bottom of prepared pan. Bake 15 minutes or until lightly browned around edges.

3. Meanwhile, dissolve coffee granules in hot water in small bowl. Pour sweetened condensed milk into medium bowl; whisk in coffee mixture. Whisk in egg and vanilla until blended. Stir in toffee bits and walnuts. Pour over crust; sprinkle with coconut.

4. Bake 25 minutes or until filling is set and coconut is toasted. Cool 5 minutes then loosen edges by running knife around sides of pan. Cool completely in pan on wire rack. Lift from pan using parchment; cut into bars.

Makes 2 to 3 dozen bars

White Chocolate and Almond Brownies

12 ounces white chocolate, coarsely chopped

1 cup (2 sticks) butter

3 eggs

1 teaspoon vanilla

¾ cup all-purpose flour

¼ teaspoon salt

½ cup slivered almonds

1. Preheat oven to 325°F. Grease and flour 9-inch square baking pan.

2. Melt white chocolate and butter in large saucepan over low heat, stirring frequently. (White chocolate may separate.) Remove from heat when chocolate is just melted. Transfer to large bowl; cool slightly.

3. Beat in eggs, one at a time, until well blended. Stir in vanilla. Stir in flour and salt just until blended. Spread batter in prepared pan; sprinkle with almonds.

4. Bake 30 minutes or until set. Cool completely in pan on wire rack.

Makes 12 to 16 brownies

Pumpkin Cheesecake Bars

1½ cups gingersnap crumbs, plus additional for garnish

6 tablespoons (¾ stick) butter, melted

2 eggs

¼ cup plus 2 tablespoons sugar, divided

2½ teaspoons vanilla, divided

11 ounces cream cheese, softened

1¼ cups canned pumpkin

1 teaspoon ground cinnamon

¼ teaspoon ground ginger

¼ teaspoon ground nutmeg

¼ teaspoon ground cloves

1 cup sour cream

1. Preheat oven to 325°F. Spray 13×9-inch baking pan with nonstick cooking spray.

2. Combine 1½ cups gingersnap crumbs and butter in small bowl; mix well. Press into bottom of prepared pan. Bake 10 minutes.

3. Meanwhile, combine eggs, ¼ cup sugar and 1½ teaspoons vanilla in food processor or blender; process 1 minute or until smooth. Add cream cheese and pumpkin; process until well blended. Stir in cinnamon, ginger, nutmeg and cloves. Pour evenly over hot crust.

4. Bake 40 minutes. Whisk sour cream, remaining 2 tablespoons sugar and 1 teaspoon vanilla in small bowl until blended. Remove cheesecake from oven; spread sour cream mixture evenly over top. Bake 5 minutes. Turn off oven; open door halfway and let cheesecake cool completely in oven. Refrigerate at least 2 hours before serving. Garnish with additional gingersnap crumbs.

Makes 2 to 3 dozen bars

Chocolate Chip Brownies

¾ cup granulated sugar

½ cup (1 stick) butter

2 tablespoons water

2 cups semisweet chocolate chips, divided

1½ teaspoons vanilla

2 eggs

1¼ cups all-purpose flour

½ teaspoon baking soda

½ teaspoon salt

Powdered sugar (optional)

1. Preheat oven to 350°F. Spray 9-inch square baking pan with nonstick cooking spray.

2. Combine granulated sugar, butter and water in medium microwavable bowl; microwave on HIGH 1½ to 2 minutes or until butter is melted. Stir in 1 cup chocolate chips; stir until chocolate is melted and mixture is smooth. Stir in vanilla. Set aside to cool 5 minutes.

3. Add eggs, one at a time, beating well after each addition. Stir in flour, baking soda and salt until blended. Stir in remaining 1 cup chocolate chips. Spread batter evenly in prepared pan.

4. Bake 25 minutes for fudgy brownies or 30 to 35 minutes for cakelike brownies. Cool completely in pan on wire rack. Sprinkle with powdered sugar, if desired.

Makes 12 to 16 brownies

Apricot Oatmeal Bars

1½ cups old-fashioned oats

1¼ cups all-purpose flour

½ cup packed brown sugar

1 teaspoon ground ginger, divided

½ teaspoon salt

½ teaspoon baking soda

½ teaspoon ground cinnamon

¾ cup (1½ sticks) butter, melted

1¼ cups apricot preserves

1. Preheat oven to 350°F. Line 8-inch square baking pan with foil.

2. Combine oats, flour, brown sugar, ½ teaspoon ginger, salt, baking soda and cinnamon in large bowl; mix well. Add butter; stir just until moistened and crumbly. Reserve 1½ cups oat mixture for topping; press remaining mixture into bottom of prepared pan.

3. Combine preserves and remaining ½ teaspoon ginger in small bowl. Spread preserves evenly over crust; sprinkle with reserved oat mixture.

4. Bake 30 minutes or until topping is golden brown. Cool completely in pan on wire rack.

Makes 12 to 16 bars

Chocolate Pecan Bars

Crust

1⅓ cups all-purpose flour

½ cup (1 stick) butter, softened

¼ cup packed brown sugar

½ teaspoon salt

Topping

¾ cup light corn syrup

3 eggs, lightly beaten

2 tablespoons butter, melted

½ teaspoon vanilla

½ teaspoon almond extract

¾ cup milk chocolate chips

¾ cup semisweet chocolate chips

¾ cup chopped pecans, toasted*

¾ cup granulated sugar

To toast pecans, spread on baking sheet. Bake in preheated 350°F oven 5 to 7 minutes or until lightly browned and fragrant, stirring frequently.

1. Preheat oven to 350°F. Spray 13×9-inch baking pan with nonstick cooking spray.

2. For crust, combine flour, ½ cup softened butter, brown sugar and salt in medium bowl; mix with fork until crumbly. Press into bottom of prepared baking pan. Bake 12 to 15 minutes or until lightly browned. Cool on wire rack 10 minutes.

3. Meanwhile, for topping, combine corn syrup, eggs, 2 tablespoons melted butter, vanilla and almond extract in large bowl; stir with fork until well blended (do not beat). Stir in chocolate chips, pecans and granulated sugar until blended. Pour over baked crust.

4. Bake 25 to 30 minutes or until toothpick inserted into center comes out clean. Cool completely in pan on wire rack.

Makes 2 to 3 dozen bars

Tip

Spray the inside of your measuring cup with nonstick cooking spray before measuring the corn syrup so it will slide out easily.

Lemon Squares

Crust

1 cup (2 sticks) butter, softened

½ cup granulated sugar

½ teaspoon salt

2 cups all-purpose flour

Filling

3 cups granulated sugar

1 cup all-purpose flour

4 eggs plus 2 egg yolks, at room temperature

⅔ cup fresh lemon juice

2 tablespoons grated lemon peel

½ teaspoon baking powder

Powdered sugar

1. Beat butter, ½ cup granulated sugar and salt in large bowl with electric mixer at medium speed about 3 minutes or until light and fluffy. Add 2 cups flour; beat at low speed just until blended.

2. Press dough into 13×9-inch baking pan, building edges up ½ inch on all sides. Refrigerate 20 minutes or until slightly firm. Preheat oven to 350°F.

3. Bake 15 to 20 minutes or until very lightly browned. Cool on wire rack 10 minutes.

4. Meanwhile, for filling, whisk 3 cups granulated sugar, 1 cup flour, eggs and egg yolks, lemon juice, lemon peel and baking powder in large bowl until well blended. Pour over crust.

5. Bake 30 to 35 minutes until filling is set. Cool completely in pan on wire rack. Cut into squares; sprinkle with powdered sugar.

Makes 2 to 3 dozen bars

White Chocolate Chunk Brownies

4 ounces unsweetened chocolate, coarsely chopped

½ cup (1 stick) butter

2 eggs

1¼ cups sugar

1 teaspoon vanilla

½ teaspoon salt

½ cup all-purpose flour

6 ounces white chocolate, cut into ¼-inch pieces

½ cup coarsely chopped walnuts (optional)

1. Preheat oven to 350°F. Line 8-inch square baking pan with parchment paper or spray with nonstick cooking spray.

2. Melt unsweetened chocolate and butter in small saucepan over very low heat, stirring frequently. Set aside to cool slightly.

3. Beat eggs in large bowl with electric mixer at medium speed 30 seconds. Gradually add sugar, beating at medium speed 4 minutes or until pale and very thick.

4. Add chocolate mixture, vanilla and salt; beat until well blended. Gradually add flour, beating at low speed just until blended. Stir in white chocolate and walnuts, if desired. Spread batter evenly in prepared pan.

5. Bake 30 minutes or until center is set and edges just begin to pull away from sides of pan. Cool completely in pan on wire rack.

Makes 12 to 16 brownies

Cranberry Walnut Granola Bars

2 packages (3 ounces each) ramen noodles, any flavor, broken into small pieces*

¾ cup all-purpose flour

1 teaspoon pumpkin pie spice

½ teaspoon baking soda

½ teaspoon salt

1 cup packed brown sugar

¼ cup (½ stick) butter, softened

2 eggs

¼ cup orange juice

1 cup chopped walnuts

½ cup dried cranberries

*Discard seasoning packets.

1. Preheat oven to 350°F. Spray 9-inch square baking pan with nonstick cooking spray.

2. Combine noodles, flour, pumpkin pie spice, baking soda and salt in medium bowl; mix well.

3. Beat brown sugar and butter in large bowl with electric mixer at medium speed about 3 minutes or until light and fluffy. Add eggs and orange juice; beat until well blended. Gradually add noodle mixture, beating at low speed just until blended. Stir in walnuts and cranberries. Spread batter evenly in prepared pan.

4. Bake 20 to 25 minutes or until toothpick inserted into center comes out clean. Cool completely in pan on wire rack.

Makes 12 to 16 bars

Shortbread Turtle Cookie Bars

1¼ cups (2½ sticks) butter, softened, divided

1 cup all-purpose flour

1 cup old-fashioned oats

1½ cups packed brown sugar, divided

1 teaspoon ground cinnamon

¼ teaspoon salt

1½ cups chopped pecans

6 ounces bittersweet or semisweet chocolate, finely chopped

4 ounces white chocolate, finely chopped

1. Preheat oven to 350°F. Position rack in center of oven.

2. Beat ½ cup butter with electric mixer at medium speed 2 minutes or until light and fluffy. Add flour, oats, ¾ cup brown sugar, cinnamon and salt; beat at low speed until coarse crumbs form. Press firmly into bottom of ungreased 13×9-inch baking pan.

3. Combine remaining ¾ cup butter and ¾ cup brown sugar in medium saucepan; cook over medium heat until mixture comes to a boil, stirring constantly. Boil 1 minute without stirring. Remove from heat; stir in pecans. Pour evenly over crust.

4. Bake 18 to 22 minutes or until caramel begins to bubble. Immediately sprinkle with bittersweet and white chocolate; swirl (do not spread) with knife after 45 seconds to 1 minute or when chocolate is slightly softened. Cool completely in pan on wire rack.

Makes 2 to 3 dozen bars

Mocha Cinnamon Blondies

1¾ cups sugar

1 cup (2 sticks) butter, melted and cooled

4 eggs

1 cup all-purpose flour

2 teaspoons instant coffee granules

1 teaspoon ground cinnamon

¼ teaspoon salt

1 cup chopped pecans

¾ cup semisweet chocolate chips

1. Preheat oven to 350°F. Spray 13×9-inch baking pan with nonstick cooking spray.

2. Beat sugar, butter and eggs in large bowl with electric mixer at medium speed about 3 minutes or until light and fluffy. Add flour, coffee granules, cinnamon and salt; beat at low speed until blended. Stir in pecans and chocolate chips. Spread batter in prepared pan.

3. Bake 30 minutes or until edges begin to pull away from sides of pan. Cool completely in pan on wire rack.

Makes 2 to 3 dozen blondies

Double Chocolate Pecan Brownies

1 cup plus 2 tablespoons all-purpose flour

¾ cup unsweetened cocoa powder

½ teaspoon baking powder

¼ teaspoon salt

1¼ cups sugar

½ cup (1 stick) butter, softened

2 eggs

1 teaspoon vanilla

½ cup semisweet chocolate chips

½ cup chopped pecans

1. Preheat oven to 350°F. Line 8-inch square baking pan with foil, extending foil over two sides of pan. Spray foil with nonstick cooking spray.

2. Combine flour, cocoa, baking powder and salt in medium bowl; mix well. Beat sugar and butter in large bowl with electric mixer at medium speed 2 to 3 minutes or until creamy. Add eggs, one at a time, beating until well blended after each addition. Beat in vanilla.

3. Gradually add flour mixture, beating at low speed just until blended. Spread batter evenly in prepared pan (batter will be very thick). Sprinkle with chocolate chips and pecans.

4. Bake about 30 minutes or until toothpick inserted into center comes out almost clean. Cool in pan 5 minutes; use foil to remove brownies to wire rack to cool completely.

Makes 12 to 16 brownies

Berry Crumble Bars

3 cups all-purpose flour

½ cup plus ⅓ cup granulated sugar, divided

½ cup packed brown sugar

1 teaspoon baking powder

1 teaspoon grated lemon peel

½ teaspoon salt

1 cup (2 sticks) cold butter, cut into small pieces

1 egg, beaten

2½ tablespoons lemon juice

1 tablespoon cornstarch

1 package (16 ounces) frozen mixed berries (do not thaw)

1. Preheat oven to 375°F. Spray 9-inch square baking pan with nonstick cooking spray or line with parchment paper and spray paper with cooking spray.

2. Combine flour, ½ cup granulated sugar, brown sugar, baking powder, lemon peel and salt in large bowl; mix well. Add butter and egg; mix with pastry blender or fingertips until crumbly dough forms. Pat one third of dough into bottom of prepared pan.

3. Combine remaining ⅓ cup granulated sugar, lemon juice and cornstarch in medium bowl; mix well. Add berries, stir gently until well blended and berries are completely coated with sugar mixture. Spread evenly over crust. Top with remaining dough, crumbling into large pieces over berry layer.

4. Bake 45 to 50 minutes or until topping is golden brown. Cool in pan on wire rack.

Makes 12 to 16 bars

Tip

Refrigerating the bars for several hours will make them easier to cut.

Cranberry Pound Cake

1½ cups sugar

1 cup (2 sticks) butter, softened

¼ teaspoon salt

¼ teaspoon ground mace or nutmeg

4 eggs

2 cups cake flour

1 cup chopped fresh or thawed frozen cranberries

1. Preheat oven to 350°F. Grease and flour 9×5-inch loaf pan.

2. Beat sugar, butter, salt and mace in large bowl with electric mixer at medium speed about 3 minutes or until light and fluffy. Add eggs, one at a time, beating well after each addition. Add flour, ½ cup at a time, beating at low speed until blended. Gently fold in cranberries. Spoon batter into prepared pan.

3. Bake 60 to 70 minutes or until toothpick inserted into center comes out clean. Cool in pan on wire rack 5 minutes. Run knife around edge of pan to loosen cake; cool 30 minutes. Remove to wire rack to cool completely.

Makes 12 servings

Note

You can make this cake when fresh or frozen cranberries aren't available. Cover 1 cup dried cranberries with hot water and let stand 10 minutes. Drain well before using.

Flourless Dark Chocolate Cake

16 ounces semisweet baking chocolate, chopped

½ cup (1 stick) butter

4 eggs, at room temperature, separated

¼ cup sugar

2 tablespoons water

½ teaspoon vanilla

½ cup seedless raspberry jam, melted (see Tip)

Whipped cream (optional)

1. Preheat oven to 350°F. Spray 9-inch springform pan with nonstick cooking spray.

2. Melt chocolate and butter in medium saucepan over low heat, stirring frequently. Remove from heat; stir in egg yolks, sugar, water and vanilla until well blended.

3. Beat egg whites in large bowl with electric mixer at medium speed. Gradually increase speed to high; beat until stiff peaks form. Fold in one third of chocolate mixture at a time until no white streaks remain. Pour batter into prepared pan; smooth top.

4. Bake 22 to 25 minutes or until center is set. Cool in pan on wire rack 30 minutes.

5. Drizzle cake with melted jam just before serving. Top with whipped cream, if desired.

Makes 8 to 10 servings

Tip

To melt jam quickly, place it in a small microwavable bowl and microwave on HIGH 30 seconds or until the jam is melted.

Praline Cheesecake

20 whole graham crackers (10 ounces total), broken into 1-inch pieces

¾ cup (1½ sticks) butter, cut into pieces

1¾ cups packed dark brown sugar, divided

4 packages (8 ounces each) cream cheese, softened

3 tablespoons maple syrup

3 tablespoons all-purpose flour

⅛ teaspoon salt

5 eggs

2 teaspoons vanilla

Bourbon Pecan Sauce (recipe follows, optional) or prepared caramel sauce

1. Preheat oven to 350°F. Combine graham crackers, butter and ½ cup brown sugar in food processor; pulse until crumbs begin to clump together.* Press into bottom and up side of 10-inch springform pan. Bake 10 minutes.

2. Beat cream cheese, maple syrup and remaining 1¼ cups brown sugar in large bowl with electric mixer at medium-high speed until smooth. Add flour and salt; beat until blended. Add eggs and vanilla; beat until well blended, scraping down side of bowl occasionally. Pour batter into crust.

3. Bake 55 to 60 minutes or until edge of cheesecake is puffed and slightly cracked and center is just set. Cool completely in pan on wire rack. Remove side of pan; cover cheesecake with plastic wrap and refrigerate overnight.

4. Prepare Bourbon Pecan Sauce, if desired. Serve with cheesecake.

*Or place graham crackers in resealable food storage bag and crush with rolling pin. Combine with brown sugar and melted butter. Proceed as directed.

Makes 12 to 16 servings

Bourbon Pecan Sauce

Combine ¾ cup packed dark brown sugar, ⅓ cup whipping cream, ¼ cup (½ stick) butter, 3 tablespoons light corn syrup and ¼ teaspoon salt in medium saucepan; bring to a boil over high heat, whisking until sugar dissolves. Reduce heat to medium; boil 1 minute without stirring. Remove from heat; stir in 3 tablespoons bourbon until blended. Stir in 1½ cups toasted pecan pieces. Let cool, stirring occasionally.

Perfect Chocolate Cake

2 cups all-purpose flour

⅔ cup unsweetened cocoa powder

1¼ teaspoons baking soda

1 teaspoon salt

¼ teaspoon baking powder

1 cup granulated sugar

¾ cup (1½ sticks) butter, softened

⅔ cup packed brown sugar

3 eggs

1 teaspoon vanilla

1⅓ cups water

Prepared chocolate frosting or powdered sugar (optional)

1. Preheat oven to 350°F. Spray 13×9-inch baking pan with nonstick cooking spray.

2. Combine flour, cocoa, baking soda, salt and baking powder in medium bowl; mix well. Beat granulated sugar, butter and brown sugar in large bowl with electric mixer at medium-high speed 2 minutes or until light and creamy. Add eggs and vanilla; beat 2 minutes. Add flour mixture alternately with water; beat just until blended. Pour batter into prepared pan.

3. Bake 25 to 35 minutes or until toothpick inserted into center comes out clean. Cool completely in pan on wire rack.

4. Frost with chocolate frosting, if desired.

Makes 12 to 16 servings

Glazed Applesauce Spice Cake

2¼ cups all-purpose flour

2 teaspoons baking soda

2 teaspoons ground cinnamon

¾ teaspoon ground nutmeg

½ teaspoon ground ginger

¼ teaspoon salt

1 cup packed brown sugar

¾ cup (1½ sticks) butter, softened

3 eggs

1½ teaspoons vanilla

1½ cups unsweetened applesauce

½ cup milk

⅔ cup chopped walnuts

⅔ cup butterscotch chips

Apple Glaze (recipe follows)

1. Preheat oven to 350°F. Grease and flour 12-cup (10-inch) bundt pan.

2. Combine flour, baking soda, cinnamon, nutmeg, ginger and salt in medium bowl; mix well.

3. Beat brown sugar and butter in large bowl with electric mixer at medium speed about 3 minutes or until light and fluffy. Beat in eggs and vanilla until well blended. Add flour mixture alternately with applesauce and milk, beginning and ending with flour mixture, beating until blended after each addition. Stir in walnuts and butterscotch chips. Pour batter into prepared pan.

4. Bake 45 to 50 minutes or until toothpick inserted near center comes out clean. Cool in pan 15 minutes; invert onto wire rack to cool completely.

5. Prepare Apple Glaze; spoon over top of cake.

Makes 12 servings

Apple Glaze

Place 1 cup sifted powdered sugar in small bowl. Stir in 2 to 3 tablespoons apple juice concentrate to make stiff glaze.

Blueberry Snack Cake

¾ cup all-purpose flour

¾ cup whole wheat flour

1 teaspoon baking soda

½ teaspoon ground cinnamon

¼ teaspoon salt

1 cup packed brown sugar

6 tablespoons (¾ stick) butter, melted

1 tablespoon white vinegar

1 teaspoon vanilla

1¼ cups sour cream

1 cup sweetened shredded coconut, toasted*

¾ cup dried blueberries

*To toast coconut, spread on small baking sheet. Bake in preheated 350°F oven 2 minutes or until lightly toasted.

1. Preheat oven to 350°F. Spray 9-inch square baking pan with nonstick cooking spray.

2. Combine all-purpose flour, whole wheat flour, baking soda, cinnamon and salt in medium bowl; mix well.

3. Combine brown sugar, butter, vinegar and vanilla in large bowl; mix well. Add flour mixture and sour cream; stir until well blended. Stir in coconut and blueberries. Spread batter in prepared pan.

4. Bake 35 minutes or until toothpick inserted into center comes out clean. Cool completely in pan on wire rack.

Makes 12 to 16 servings

Molten Cinnamon Chocolate Cakes

6 ounces semisweet chocolate

¾ cup (1½ sticks) butter

1½ cups powdered sugar, plus additional for garnish

4 eggs

6 tablespoons all-purpose flour

1½ teaspoons vanilla

¾ teaspoon ground cinnamon

1. Preheat oven to 425°F. Spray six jumbo (3½-inch) muffin cups or six 1-cup custard cups with nonstick cooking spray.

2. Combine chocolate and butter in medium microwavable bowl; microwave on HIGH 1½ minutes or until melted and smooth, stirring every 30 seconds. Whisk in 1½ cups powdered sugar, eggs, flour, vanilla and cinnamon until well blended. Pour batter into prepared muffin cups, filling two thirds full.

3. Bake 13 minutes or until cakes spring back when lightly touched but centers are soft. Let stand 1 minute. Loosen sides of cakes with knife; gently lift out and invert onto serving plates. Sprinkle with additional powdered sugar. Serve immediately.

Makes 6 servings

Classic Yellow Cake

Cake

2¾ cups cake flour

1 tablespoon baking powder

¾ teaspoon salt

¾ cup (1½ sticks) butter, softened

1¾ cups granulated sugar

3 eggs, at room temperature

2 egg yolks, at room temperature

¼ cup vegetable oil

2 teaspoons vanilla

1 cup whole milk, at room temperature

Frosting

1 cup (2 sticks) butter, softened

4 cups powdered sugar, sifted

2 teaspoons vanilla*

2 to 3 tablespoons milk

Multicolored sprinkles (optional)

For brighter white frosting, use clear vanilla extract (available in many supermarkets and specialty stores). The dark color of standard vanilla extract will make the frosting an off-white color.

1. For cake, preheat oven to 350°F. Spray two 9-inch round cake pans with nonstick cooking spray; line bottoms with parchment paper.

2. Sift flour, baking powder and salt into medium bowl. Beat ¾ cup butter in large bowl with electric mixer at medium speed 2 minutes or until creamy. Add granulated sugar; beat about 3 minutes or until light and fluffy. Add eggs and egg yolks, one at a time, beating well after each addition and scraping down side of bowl several times. Beat in oil and 2 teaspoons vanilla until blended. Alternately add flour mixture and 1 cup milk, beginning and ending with flour mixture; beat at low speed just until blended. Pour batter into prepared pans.

3. Bake 28 to 30 minutes or until toothpick inserted into centers comes out with few moist crumbs. Cool in pans 10 minutes; remove to wire racks to cool completely.

4. For frosting, beat 1 cup butter in large bowl with electric mixer at medium speed about 3 minutes or until smooth and creamy and lightened in color. Add powdered sugar, ½ cup at a time, beating at medium-high speed until well blended after each addition, scraping down side of bowl occasionally. Add 2 teaspoons vanilla; beat until blended. Add 2 tablespoons milk; beat at medium-high speed 3 minutes or until light and fluffy. If frosting is too thick, add additional milk, 1 teaspoon at a time; beat until well blended.

5. Place one cake layer on serving plate; spread with 1 cup frosting. Top with remaining cake layer; frost top and side of cake. Top with sprinkles, if desired.

Makes 12 servings

Chocolate Marble Cake

2½ cups all-purpose flour

2 cups sugar, divided

2 teaspoons baking powder

1¼ teaspoons baking soda, divided

1 teaspoon salt

1⅔ cups buttermilk

¾ cup (1½ sticks) butter, softened, cut into small pieces

3 eggs, beaten

1 tablespoon vanilla

⅓ cup unsweetened cocoa powder

¼ cup water

½ teaspoon espresso powder

Chocolate Glaze (recipe follows)

1. Preheat oven to 375°F. Grease and flour 12-cup (10-inch) bundt pan.

2. Combine flour, 1⅔ cups sugar, baking powder, 1 teaspoon baking soda and salt in large bowl; mix well. Add buttermilk, butter, eggs, and vanilla; beat with electric mixer at low speed 1 minute. Beat at medium speed 2 to 3 minutes or until well blended. Remove ¾ cup batter to medium bowl.

3. Combine remaining ⅓ cup sugar, ¼ teaspoon baking soda, cocoa, water and espresso powder in small bowl; stir until blended and smooth. Add to ¾ cup reserved batter; mix well. Spoon vanilla batter into prepared pan; drop spoonfuls of chocolate batter over vanilla batter. Swirl with knife or skewer to marbleize.

4. Bake 40 to 45 minutes or until toothpick inserted near center comes out clean. Cool in pan 15 minutes; invert onto wire rack to cool completely.

5. Prepare Chocolate Glaze; drizzle over cake. Let stand until set.

Makes 12 servings

Chocolate Glaze

Combine ¼ cup unsweetened cocoa powder, 3 tablespoons light corn syrup and 1½ tablespoons water in small saucepan; cook and stir over medium heat until thickened. Remove from heat; stir in 1 cup powdered sugar and ¼ teaspoon vanilla until well blended and smooth.

Carrot Cake

2 cups all-purpose flour

2 teaspoons baking soda

2 teaspoons ground cinnamon, plus additional for garnish

1 teaspoon salt

2 cups sugar

1 cup vegetable oil

4 eggs

1 teaspoon vanilla

3 cups finely grated carrots (about 5 medium)

1 cup shredded coconut

1 can (8 ounces) crushed pineapple

1 cup chopped walnuts

Cream Cheese Frosting (recipe follows)

1. Preheat oven to 350°F. Spray 13×9-inch baking pan with nonstick cooking spray.

2. Combine flour, baking soda, 2 teaspoons cinnamon and salt in medium bowl; mix well. Beat sugar and oil in large bowl until well blended. Add eggs, one at a time, beating well after each addition. Beat in vanilla. Add flour mixture; stir until blended. Add carrots, coconut, pineapple and walnuts; stir just until blended. Pour batter into prepared pan.

3. Bake 45 to 50 minutes or until toothpick inserted into center comes out clean. Cool completely in pan on wire rack.

4. Prepare Cream Cheese Frosting; spread over cake. Sprinkle with additional cinnamon, if desired.

Makes 12 to 16 servings

Cream Cheese Frosting

Beat 1 package (8 ounces) softened cream cheese, ½ cup (1 stick) softened butter and pinch of salt in large bowl with electric mixer at medium speed 3 minutes or until light and creamy. Add 1½ cups powdered sugar, 1 tablespoon milk and 1 teaspoon vanilla; beat at low speed until blended. Beat at medium speed 2 minutes or until frosting is smooth. Add additional milk for softer frosting, if desired.

Fudgy Chocolate Pudding Cake

1 cup all-purpose flour

1 cup granulated sugar, divided

½ cup unsweetened cocoa powder, divided

2 teaspoons baking powder

¼ teaspoon salt

½ cup milk

6 tablespoons (¾ stick) butter, melted

1 teaspoon vanilla

⅔ cup packed dark brown sugar

1¼ cups hot water

Vanilla ice cream (optional)

1. Preheat oven to 350°F. Spray 8-inch square baking pan with nonstick cooking spray.

2. Combine flour, ¾ cup granulated sugar, ¼ cup cocoa, baking powder and salt in medium bowl; mix well. Beat in milk, butter and vanilla until blended. Spoon batter into prepared pan.

3. Combine remaining ¼ cup granulated sugar, ¼ cup cocoa and brown sugar in small bowl; mix well. Sprinkle evenly over batter. Carefully pour hot water over batter. *Do not stir.*

4. Bake 25 to 35 minutes or until cake jiggles slightly when gently shaken. Let stand 15 minutes. Serve with ice cream, if desired.

Makes 8 servings

Toffee Crunch Cheesecake

Crust

8 ounces chocolate cookies or vanilla wafers, crushed

¼ cup (½ stick) butter, melted

Filling

3 packages (8 ounces each) cream cheese, softened

½ cup granulated sugar

¼ cup packed brown sugar

3 eggs

1¾ cups (10-ounce package) toffee baking bits, divided

1¼ teaspoons vanilla

Whipped cream (optional)

1. Preheat oven to 350°F. For crust, combine cookie crumbs and butter in medium bowl; mix well. Press firmly into bottom of 9-inch springform pan.

2. For filling, beat cream cheese, granulated sugar and brown sugar in large bowl with electric mixer at medium speed about 3 minutes or until smooth and creamy. Add eggs, one at a time, beating well after each addition. Reserve 1 tablespoon toffee bits for garnish; gently stir remaining toffee bits and vanilla into batter. Pour batter into crust.

3. Bake 45 to 50 minutes or until almost set. Remove to wire rack. Carefully run knife around edge of pan to loosen cheesecake. Cool completely; remove side of pan. Cover and refrigerate until cold.

4. Just before serving, top with whipped cream, if desired. Garnish with reserved toffee bits.

Makes 12 servings

Cherry Coconut Cheese Coffeecake

2½ cups all-purpose flour

¾ cup sugar

½ teaspoon baking powder

½ teaspoon baking soda

6 ounces cream cheese, softened, divided

¾ cup milk

2 eggs, divided

2 tablespoons vegetable oil

1 teaspoon vanilla

½ cup flaked coconut

¾ cup cherry preserves

2 tablespoons butter, cut into small pieces

1. Preheat oven to 350°F. Grease and flour 9-inch springform pan.

2. Combine flour and sugar in large bowl; mix well. Reserve ½ cup flour mixture in small bowl; set aside. Stir baking powder and baking soda into remaining flour mixture. Cut in half of cream cheese with pastry blender or two knives until mixture resembles coarse crumbs.

3. Whisk milk, 1 egg and oil in medium bowl until well blended. Add to cream cheese mixture; stir just until moistened. Spread batter on bottom and 1 inch up side of prepared pan. Combine remaining cream cheese, egg and vanilla in small bowl; stir until smooth. Pour over batter, spreading to within 1 inch of edge. Sprinkle with coconut; top with spoonfuls of preserves.

4. Cut butter into reserved flour mixture with pastry blender or mix with fingertips until mixture resembles coarse crumbs. Sprinkle over preserves.

5. Bake 55 to 60 minutes or until golden brown and toothpick inserted into crust comes out clean. Cool in pan on wire rack 15 minutes. Remove side of pan; serve warm.

Makes 10 servings

Rich Chocolate Bundt Cake

Cake

- 1 **cup water**
- ¾ **cup (1½ sticks) butter, plus additional for pan**
- ¾ **cup unsweetened cocoa powder, plus additional for pan**
- 1 **teaspoon espresso powder**
- 2 **cups all-purpose flour**
- 2 **cups sugar**
- 1 **teaspoon baking powder**
- 1 **teaspoon baking soda**
- ¾ **teaspoon salt**
- 2 **eggs, at room temperature**
- ¼ **cup vegetable oil**
- ½ **cup sour cream, at room temperature**
- 1½ **teaspoons vanilla**

Ganache

- ½ **cup whipping cream**
- ¾ **cup semisweet chocolate chips**

1. Preheat oven to 350°F. For cake, generously grease 12-cup (10-inch) bundt pan with butter; dust with cocoa.

2. Combine water, ¾ cup butter, ¾ cup cocoa and espresso powder in medium saucepan; heat over low heat until butter is melted and mixture is smooth, stirring frequently. Remove from heat; set aside to cool slightly.

3. Combine flour, sugar, baking powder, baking soda and salt in large bowl; mix well.

4. Add eggs and oil to cocoa mixture; whisk until blended. Whisk in sour cream and vanilla until well blended. Add to flour mixture; stir until well blended. Pour batter into prepared pan.

5. Bake 40 to 45 minutes or until toothpick inserted near center comes out clean. Cool in pan 10 minutes; invert onto wire rack to cool completely.

6. For ganache, heat cream to a simmer in microwave or on stovetop. Add chocolate chips; let stand 5 minutes. Stir until smooth. Drizzle over cake.

Makes 12 servings

Apple Cake

2½ cups all-purpose flour

2 teaspoons ground cinnamon, divided

1 teaspoon baking powder

1 teaspoon baking soda

1 teaspoon salt

¼ teaspoon ground nutmeg

1¼ cups granulated sugar, divided

1 cup (2 sticks) butter, softened

¾ cup packed brown sugar

2 eggs

1 teaspoon vanilla

1 cup buttermilk

3 cups chopped peeled apples

1 cup chopped nuts

1. Preheat oven to 350°F. Spray 13×9-inch baking pan with nonstick cooking spray.

2. Combine flour, 1 teaspoon cinnamon, baking powder, baking soda, salt and nutmeg in medium bowl; mix well.

3. Beat ¾ cup granulated sugar, butter, brown sugar, eggs and vanilla in large bowl with electric mixer at medium speed about 3 minutes or until creamy. Beat in buttermilk until blended. Gradually add flour mixture; beating at low speed until blended. Stir in apples. Pour batter into prepared pan.

4. Combine remaining ½ cup granulated sugar, 1 teaspoon cinnamon and nuts in small bowl; mix well. Sprinkle over batter.

5. Bake 35 to 40 minutes or until toothpick inserted into center comes out clean. Cool completely in pan on wire rack.

Makes 12 to 16 servings

Creamy Chocolate Cheesecake

Chocolate Crumb Crust
(recipe follows)

2 cups semisweet
chocolate chips

¾ cup whipping cream

3 packages (8 ounces
each) cream cheese,
softened

¾ cup packed
brown sugar

3 eggs

¼ cup unsweetened
cocoa powder

1 teaspoon vanilla

Whipped cream
(optional)

Crushed peppermint
candy (optional)

1. Preheat oven to 325°F. Prepare Chocolate Crumb Crust.

2. Heat chocolate chips and cream in medium saucepan over low heat until chocolate is melted and mixture is smooth, stirring frequently. Set aside to cool slightly.

3. Beat cream cheese in large bowl with electric mixer at medium speed until fluffy. Add brown sugar; beat about 3 minutes or until light and fluffy. Add eggs, one at a time, beating well after each addition. Stir in cocoa and vanilla. Beat in melted chocolate mixture at low speed, scraping side of bowl frequently. Pour batter into crust.

4. Bake 45 to 50 minutes or until center is just set. Remove to wire rack. Carefully run knife around edge of pan to loosen cheesecake. Cool completely. Refrigerate several hours or overnight.

5. Remove side of pan. Top with whipped cream and candy, if desired.

Makes 12 servings

Chocolate Crumb Crust

Preheat oven to 325°F. Combine 1 cup chocolate wafer crumbs and 3 tablespoons melted butter in small bowl; mix well. Press into bottom of 9-inch springform pan. Bake 10 minutes. Cool on wire rack while preparing filling.

Rustic Cranberry Pear Galette

¼ **cup sugar, divided**

1 **tablespoon plus
1 teaspoon cornstarch**

2 **teaspoons ground
cinnamon or apple pie
spice**

4 **cups thinly sliced
peeled Bartlett pears**

¼ **cup dried cranberries**

1 **teaspoon vanilla**

¼ **teaspoon almond
extract (optional)**

1 **refrigerated pie crust,
at room temperature
(half of 14-ounce
package)**

1 **egg white**

1 **tablespoon water**

1. Preheat oven to 450°F. Line baking sheet or pizza pan with parchment paper or spray with nonstick cooking spray.

2. Reserve 1 teaspoon sugar. Combine remaining sugar, cornstarch and cinnamon in medium bowl; mix well. Add pears, cranberries, vanilla and almond extract, if desired; toss to coat.

3. Place crust on prepared baking sheet. Spoon pear mixture into center of crust, spreading to within 2 inches of edge. Fold edge of crust in towards center over pear mixture, overlapping or pleating as necessary.

4. Whisk egg white and water in small bowl until well blended. Brush over crust; sprinkle with reserved 1 teaspoon sugar.

5. Bake 25 minutes or until pears are tender and crust is golden brown.* Cool on baking sheet on wire rack 30 minutes. Serve warm or at room temperature.

If edge browns too quickly, cover loosely with foil after 15 minutes of baking.

Makes 8 servings

Caribbean Coconut Pie

1 unbaked deep-dish
  9-inch pie crust

1 can (14 ounces)
  sweetened condensed
  milk

¾ cup flaked coconut

2 eggs

½ cup hot water

2 teaspoons grated
  lime peel

Juice of 1 lime

¼ teaspoon salt

⅛ teaspoon ground
  red pepper

Whipped cream
(optional)

1. Preheat oven to 400°F. Prick holes in bottom of crust with fork. Bake 10 minutes or until lightly browned. Cool on wire rack 15 minutes.

2. *Reduce oven temperature to 350°F.* Whisk sweetened condensed milk, coconut, eggs, hot water, lime peel, lime juice, salt and red pepper in large bowl until well blended. Pour into crust.

3. Bake 30 minutes or until knife inserted into center comes out clean. Cool completely on wire rack.

4. Top with whipped cream, if desired.

Makes 8 servings

Apple Buttermilk Pie

2 medium Granny Smith
  apples

3 eggs

1½ cups sugar, divided

1 cup buttermilk

⅓ cup butter, melted

2 tablespoons all-purpose
  flour

2 teaspoons vanilla

2 teaspoons ground
  cinnamon, divided,
  plus additional for
  garnish

¾ teaspoon ground
  nutmeg, divided

1 (9-inch) unbaked
  pie crust

Whipped cream
(optional)

1. Preheat oven to 350°F. Peel and core apples; cut into small pieces. Place apples in medium bowl; cover with cold water and set aside.

2. Whisk eggs in medium bowl. Add all but 1 teaspoon sugar, buttermilk, butter, flour, vanilla, 1 teaspoon cinnamon and ½ teaspoon nutmeg; whisk until well blended.

3. Drain apples well; place in unbaked crust. Pour buttermilk mixture over apples. Combine remaining 1 teaspoon sugar, 1 teaspoon cinnamon and ¼ teaspoon nutmeg in small bowl; sprinkle over top.

4. Bake 50 to 60 minutes or until knife inserted into center comes out clean. Serve warm or at room temperature. Garnish with whipped cream and additional cinnamon.

Makes 8 servings

Praline Pumpkin Tart

1¼ cups all-purpose flour

1 tablespoon granulated sugar

¾ teaspoon salt, divided

¼ cup cold shortening, cut into small pieces

¼ cup (½ stick) cold butter, cut into small pieces

3 to 4 tablespoons cold water

1 can (15 ounces) pure pumpkin

1 can (12 ounces) evaporated milk

⅔ cup packed brown sugar

2 eggs

1 teaspoon ground cinnamon

½ teaspoon ground ginger

¼ teaspoon ground cloves

Praline Topping (recipe follows)

1. Combine flour, granulated sugar and ¼ teaspoon salt in large bowl. Cut in shortening and butter with pastry blender or fingers until coarse crumbs form. Sprinkle with water, 1 tablespoon at a time; mix with fork until mixture holds together. Shape dough into a ball; wrap in plastic wrap. Refrigerate about 1 hour or until chilled.

2. Roll out dough into 13×9-inch rectangle on lightly floured surface. Press into bottom and up sides of 11×7-inch baking dish. Cover with plastic wrap; refrigerate 30 minutes.

3. Preheat oven to 400°F. Pierce crust with fork at ¼-inch intervals. Line baking dish with foil; fill with dried beans, uncooked rice or ceramic pie weights. Bake 10 minutes or until set.

4. Remove crust from oven; gently remove foil and beans. Bake 5 minutes or until crust is golden brown. Cool completely on wire rack.

5. Whisk pumpkin, evaporated milk, brown sugar, eggs, cinnamon, remaining ½ teaspoon salt, ginger and cloves in large bowl until well blended. Pour into cooled crust. Bake 35 minutes.

6. Meanwhile, prepare Praline Topping. Sprinkle topping over tart. Bake 15 minutes or until knife inserted 1 inch from center comes out clean. Cool completely on wire rack.

Makes 8 servings

Praline Topping

Combine ⅓ cup packed brown sugar, ⅓ cup chopped pecans and ⅓ cup quick oats in small bowl. Cut in 1 tablespoon softened butter with pastry blender or mix with fingertips until coarse crumbs form.

Sweet Potato Honey Pie

1 refrigerated pie crust
(half of 14-ounce
package)

1 can (29 ounces) cut-up
sweet potatoes

2 eggs

⅔ cup honey

2 tablespoons butter,
melted

¾ teaspoon ground
cinnamon

½ teaspoon salt

½ teaspoon ground ginger

¼ teaspoon ground cloves

1 cup whole milk

Whipped cream

Ground nutmeg
(optional)

1. Preheat oven to 425°F. Line 9-inch pie plate with crust; flute edge.

2. Drain sweet potatoes, reserving 2 tablespoons liquid. Combine sweet potatoes and liquid in food processor; pulse until smooth. Measure 2½ cups for pie; reserve any remaining purée for another use.

3. Whisk eggs in large bowl. Add sweet potato purée, honey, butter, cinnamon, salt, ginger and cloves; whisk until well blended. Stir in milk. Pour into crust.

4. Bake 15 minutes. *Reduce oven temperature to 350°F.* Bake 40 to 45 minutes or until filling is puffy. Cool on wire rack. Serve at room temperature or chilled with whipped cream. Garnish with nutmeg.

Makes 6 to 8 servings

Plum Walnut Pie

Oat Streusel
(recipe follows)

8 cups thinly sliced plums

⅓ cup granulated sugar

⅓ cup packed brown
sugar

3 to 4 tablespoons
all-purpose flour

1 tablespoon honey

½ teaspoon ground
cinnamon

¼ teaspoon ground ginger

⅛ teaspoon salt

1 refrigerated pie crust
(half of 14-ounce
package) or ½ recipe
Rich Pie Dough
(page 180)

½ cup candied walnuts

*Candied walnuts may be found
in the baking section of the
supermarket, or they may be
found in the produce section
with other salad toppings.*

1. Prepare Oat Streusel; set aside.

2. Preheat oven to 425°F. Combine plums, granulated sugar, brown sugar, 3 tablespoons flour (use 4 tablespoons if plums are very juicy), honey, cinnamon, ginger and salt in large bowl; toss to coat.

3. Line 9-inch pie plate with crust; flute edge. (If preparing Rich Pie Dough, roll out dough into 12-inch circle on floured surface before lining pie plate with dough.). Spread plum mixture evenly in crust; sprinkle with Oat Streusel. Place pie on baking sheet.

4. Bake 15 minutes. *Reduce oven temperature to 350°F.* Sprinkle pie with walnuts. Bake 30 minutes. Loosely tent pie with foil. Bake 30 minutes or until filling is bubbly and crust is golden brown. Let stand at least 30 minutes before serving.

Makes 8 servings

Oat Streusel

Combine ¼ cup all-purpose flour, ¼ cup old-fashioned oats, ¼ cup granulated sugar, ¼ cup packed brown sugar and ⅛ teaspoon salt in medium bowl. Cut in ¼ cup (½ stick) cubed butter with pastry blender or mix with fingertips until mixture resembles coarse crumbs.

Cherry Frangipane Tart

1 refrigerated pie crust (half of 14-ounce package)

⅔ cup slivered almonds

½ cup all-purpose flour

¼ cup powdered sugar

½ cup (1 stick) butter, softened, cut into pieces

2 eggs

1¾ cups pitted frozen sweet cherries

Fresh mint leaves (optional)

1. Preheat oven to 450°F. Let crust stand at room temperature 15 minutes.

2. Line 9-inch tart pan with crust; cover with parchment paper. Fill with dried beans or pie weights and bake 10 minutes. Remove from oven; carefully remove parchment and beans. *Reduce oven temperature to 350°F.*

3. Combine almonds, flour and powdered sugar in food processor; process until almonds are finely ground. Add butter; pulse to blend.

4. With motor running, add eggs, one at a time; process until blended. Pour into baked crust; smooth top. Sprinkle with cherries.

5. Bake 35 minutes or until set. Cool completely in pan on wire rack. Garnish with mint.

Makes 6 to 8 servings

Lemon Chess Pie

1 refrigerated pie crust (half of 14-ounce package)

3 eggs

2 egg yolks

1¾ cups sugar

½ cup half-and-half

⅓ cup lemon juice

¼ cup (½ stick) butter, melted

3 tablespoons grated lemon peel, plus additional for garnish

2 tablespoons all-purpose flour

Whipped cream (optional)

1. Preheat oven to 325°F. Let crust stand at room temperature 15 minutes. Line 9-inch pie plate with crust; flute edge.

2. Whisk eggs and egg yolks in large bowl. Add sugar, half-and-half, lemon juice, butter, 3 tablespoons lemon peel and flour; whisk until well blended. Pour into crust.

3. Bake 40 minutes or until almost set. Cool completely on wire rack. Refrigerate 2 hours or until ready to serve. Top with whipped cream, if desired; garnish with additional lemon peel.

Makes 8 servings

Tip

To determine doneness, carefully shake the pie; it is done when only the center 2 inches jiggle.

Cranberry Apple Nut Pie

Rich Pie Dough
(recipe follows)

1 cup sugar

3 tablespoons all-purpose
flour

¼ teaspoon salt

4 cups sliced peeled tart
apples (4 large apples)

2 cups fresh cranberries

½ cup golden raisins

½ cup coarsely chopped
pecans

1 tablespoon grated
lemon peel

2 tablespoons butter,
cut into small pieces

1 egg, beaten

1. Preheat oven to 425°F. Prepare Rich Pie Dough.

2. Roll out one disc of dough into 11-inch circle on floured surface. Line 9-inch pie plate with dough.

3. Combine sugar, flour and salt in large bowl; mix well. Stir in apples, cranberries, raisins, pecans and lemon peel; toss to coat. Pour into crust; dot with butter.

4. Roll out remaining disc of dough into 11-inch circle. Place over filling; trim excess dough. Seal and flute edge. Cut three slits in center of top crust. Lightly brush top crust with egg.

5. Bake 35 minutes or until crust is golden brown and apples are tender when pierced with fork. Cool on wire rack 15 minutes. Serve warm or cool completely.

Makes 8 servings

Rich Pie Dough

2 cups all-purpose flour

¼ teaspoon salt

6 tablespoons (¾ stick)
cold butter, cubed

6 tablespoons shortening,
cubed

6 to 8 tablespoons cold
water

Combine flour and salt in medium bowl. Cut in butter and shortening with pastry blender or two knives until mixture resembles coarse crumbs. Sprinkle with water, 1 tablespoon at a time, mixing until dough forms. Divide dough in half. Shape each half into a disc; wrap in plastic wrap. Refrigerate 30 minutes.

Makes dough for 9-inch double-crust pie

Note
For a single-crust pie, cut the recipe in half.

Almond Custard Pie

1½ cups all-purpose flour

½ cup plus 1 tablespoon granulated sugar, divided

½ teaspoon salt, divided

½ cup (1 stick) butter, melted

3 eggs

¼ teaspoon ground cinnamon

2 cups half-and-half

½ teaspoon almond extract

1 tablespoon butter

¾ cup sliced almonds

2 tablespoons packed dark brown sugar

1. Preheat oven to 425°F. Combine flour, 1 tablespoon granulated sugar and ¼ teaspoon salt in large bowl; mix well. Gradually add ½ cup melted butter, stirring until dough forms.

2. Place dough in 9-inch pie plate; press onto bottom and up side, forming high rim. Place on baking sheet. Bake 5 minutes. (It is not necessary to weigh down crust.) *Reduce oven temperature to 325°F.*

3. Whisk eggs in large bowl. Add remaining ½ cup granulated sugar, ¼ teaspoon salt and cinnamon; whisk until well blended. Whisk in half-and-half and almond extract.

4. Melt 1 tablespoon butter in medium skillet over medium heat. Add almonds; cook and stir 2 minutes or until golden brown. Remove from heat; cool slightly. Pour custard into crust. Spoon almonds over custard; sprinkle with brown sugar.

5. Bake 30 minutes or until set. Cool 30 minutes on wire rack. Serve at room temperature or chilled.

Makes 8 servings

Note

You can substitute an unbaked 9-inch deep-dish pie crust for the homemade crust. Let the crust stand at room temperature 15 minutes. Prick holes in the bottom of the crust with a fork; bake 5 minutes as directed for the homemade crust.

Ginger Plum Tart

1 refrigerated pie crust (half of 14-ounce package)

1¾ pounds plums, cut into ½-inch slices

½ cup plus 1 teaspoon sugar, divided

1½ tablespoons all-purpose flour

1½ teaspoons ground ginger

¼ teaspoon ground cinnamon

⅛ teaspoon salt

1 egg

2 teaspoons water

1. Preheat oven to 400°F. Let crust stand at room temperature 10 minutes.

2. Combine plums, ½ cup sugar, flour, ginger, cinnamon and salt in large bowl; toss to coat.

3. Roll out crust into 14-inch circle on lightly floured surface. Transfer to large (10-inch) ovenproof skillet. Mound plum mixture in center of crust, leaving 2-inch border around fruit. Fold edge of crust in towards center over filling, pleating as necessary and gently pressing crust into fruit to adhere.

4. Beat egg and water in small bowl; brush over crust. Sprinkle with remaining 1 teaspoon sugar.*

5. Bake about 45 minutes or until crust is golden brown. Cool on wire rack. Serve warm or at room temperature.

*To add sparkle and extra crunch to the tart, use sparkling or coarse sugar to sprinkle on top instead of granulated sugar.

Makes 6 to 8 servings

Fancy Fudge Pie

1 cup chocolate wafer
    crumbs

⅓ cup butter, melted

1⅓ cups semisweet
    chocolate chips

¾ cup packed
    brown sugar

½ cup (1 stick) butter,
    softened

3 eggs

1 cup chopped pecans

½ cup all-purpose flour

1 teaspoon vanilla

½ teaspoon instant
    espresso powder

Whipped cream
    (optional)

Chocolate syrup
    (optional)

1. Preheat oven to 375°F. Combine wafer crumbs and ⅓ cup melted butter in small bowl; mix well. Press into bottom and up side of 9-inch pie plate. Bake 5 minutes. Cool completely on wire rack.

2. Place chocolate chips in small microwavable bowl; microwave on HIGH 1 minute or until melted and smooth, stirring after 30 seconds. Set aside to cool slightly.

3. Beat brown sugar and ½ cup softened butter in large bowl with electric mixer at medium speed about 3 minutes or until light and fluffy. Add eggs, one at a time, beating well after each addition. Stir in melted chocolate, pecans, flour, vanilla and espresso powder until blended. Pour into crust.

4. Bake 30 minutes or until set. Cool completely on wire rack. Cover and refrigerate 2 hours or until ready to serve. Garnish with whipped cream and chocolate syrup.

Makes 8 servings

Peach Cherry Pie

- 1 refrigerated pie crust (half of 14-ounce package)
- Streusel Topping (recipe follows)
- ¾ cup granulated sugar
- 3 tablespoons quick-cooking tapioca
- 1 teaspoon grated lemon peel
- ½ teaspoon ground cinnamon
- ⅛ teaspoon salt
- 4 cups peach slices (about 7 medium)
- 2 cups Bing cherries, pitted
- 1 tablespoon lemon juice
- 2 tablespoons butter, cut into small pieces

1. Preheat oven to 375°F. Let crust stand at room temperature 15 minutes.

2. Prepare Streusel Topping. Line 9-inch pie plate with crust; flute edge.

3. Combine granulated sugar, tapioca, lemon peel, cinnamon and salt in large bowl; mix well. Add peaches, cherries and lemon juice; toss to coat. Spread evenly in crust; dot with butter. Sprinkle with Streusel Topping.

4. Bake 40 minutes or until filling is bubbly. Cool on wire rack 15 minutes. Serve warm or at room temperature.

Makes 6 to 8 servings

Streusel Topping

Combine ¾ cup old-fashioned oats, ⅓ cup all-purpose flour, ⅓ cup packed brown sugar and ¾ teaspoon ground cinnamon in medium bowl; mix well. Stir in 4 tablespoons (½ stick) melted butter until mixture resembles coarse crumbs.

Spiced Pumpkin Pie

Pie dough for single-crust 9-inch pie

1 can (15 ounces) pure pumpkin

¾ cup packed brown sugar

2 teaspoons ground cinnamon

¾ teaspoon ground ginger

½ teaspoon ground nutmeg, plus additional for garnish

¼ teaspoon salt

⅛ teaspoon ground cloves

4 eggs, lightly beaten

1 cup light cream or half-and-half

1 teaspoon vanilla

Whipped cream (optional)

1. Preheat oven to 400°F. Roll out dough into 12-inch circle on lightly floured surface. Line 9-inch pie plate with dough; trim and flute edge.

2. Whisk pumpkin, brown sugar, cinnamon, ginger, ½ teaspoon nutmeg, salt and cloves in large bowl until well blended. Add eggs; whisk until blended. Gradually whisk in cream and vanilla until well blended. Pour into crust.

3. Bake 40 to 45 minutes or until knife inserted near center comes out clean. Cool completely on wire rack. Serve warm or at room temperature; garnish with whipped cream and additional nutmeg.

Makes 8 servings

Chocolate Walnut Toffee Tart

- 2 cups all-purpose flour
- 1¼ cups plus 3 tablespoons sugar, divided
- ¾ cup (1½ sticks) butter, cut into pieces
- 2 egg yolks
- 1¼ cups whipping cream
- 1 teaspoon ground cinnamon
- 2 teaspoons vanilla
- 2 cups coarsely chopped walnuts
- 1¼ cups semisweet chocolate chips or chunks, divided

1. Preheat oven to 325°F. Line baking sheet with foil.

2. Combine flour and 3 tablespoons sugar in food processor; pulse just until blended. Scatter butter over flour mixture; process 20 seconds. Add egg yolks; process 10 seconds (mixture may be crumbly).

3. Press dough firmly into ungreased 10-inch tart pan with removable bottom or 9- or 10-inch pie plate. Bake 10 minutes or until surface is no longer shiny. Place tart pan on prepared baking sheet. *Increase oven temperature to 375°F.*

4. Combine remaining 1¼ cups sugar, cream and cinnamon in large saucepan; bring to a boil over medium-high heat. Reduce heat to medium-low; simmer 10 minutes, stirring frequently. Remove from heat; stir in vanilla.

5. Sprinkle walnuts and 1 cup chocolate chips evenly over crust. Pour cream mixture over top.

6. Bake 35 to 40 minutes or until crust is lightly browned and filling is bubbly. Cool completely on wire rack.

7. Place remaining ¼ cup chocolate chips in small resealable food storage bag. Microwave on HIGH 20 seconds; knead bag until chocolate is melted. Cut small hole in one corner of bag; drizzle chocolate over tart.

Makes 12 servings

Warm Mixed Berry Pie

2 packages (12 ounces each) frozen mixed berries

⅓ cup sugar

3 tablespoons cornstarch

2 teaspoons grated orange peel

¼ teaspoon ground ginger

1 refrigerated pie crust (half of 14-ounce package)

1. Preheat oven to 350°F.

2. Combine berries, sugar, cornstarch, orange peel and ginger in large bowl; toss gently to coat. Spoon into large (10-inch) ovenproof skillet.

3. Roll out crust into 12-inch circle on lightly floured surface. Place over fruit mixture in skillet; flute edge as desired. Cut several slits in crust to allow steam to escape.

4. Bake 1 hour or until crust is golden brown. Let stand 1 hour before serving.

Makes 8 servings

Delicious Desserts

Bananas Foster Crisp

¾ cup packed dark brown
    sugar, divided

6 tablespoons (¾ stick)
    butter, divided

3 tablespoons dark rum

½ teaspoon ground
    cinnamon

¼ teaspoon grated
    nutmeg

8 medium bananas (firm,
    yellow, no spots), cut
    into ½-inch slices
    (about 6 cups)

½ cup all-purpose flour

½ cup chopped pecans

¼ teaspoon salt

    Vanilla ice cream
    (optional)

1. Position oven rack in lower third of oven. Preheat oven to 375°F. Spray 8-inch round or square baking dish with nonstick cooking spray.

2. Combine ½ cup brown sugar and 2 tablespoons butter in small saucepan; cook and stir over medium heat about 3 minutes or until butter is melted and sugar is dissolved. Gradually add rum, cinnamon and nutmeg (mixture will spatter); cook 1 minute, stirring constantly. Pour mixture into large bowl. Add bananas; toss to coat. Spoon into prepared baking dish.

3. Combine flour, pecans, remaining ¼ cup brown sugar and salt in medium bowl; mix well. Cut remaining 4 tablespoons butter into small pieces. Add to flour mixture; mix with fingertips until mixture forms coarse crumbs. Sprinkle over banana mixture.

4. Bake 40 minutes or until filling is bubbly and topping is golden brown. Let stand 1 hour before serving. Serve with ice cream, if desired.

Makes 6 to 8 servings

Ginger Pear Cobbler

7 firm ripe d'Anjou pears (about 3½ pounds), peeled and cut into ½-inch pieces

⅓ cup packed brown sugar

1 cup plus 2 tablespoons all-purpose flour, divided

2 tablespoons lemon juice

2 teaspoons ground ginger, divided

½ teaspoon ground cinnamon

⅛ teaspoon ground nutmeg

¼ cup granulated sugar

1½ teaspoons baking powder

¼ teaspoon salt

¼ cup (½ stick) butter, cut into small pieces

¼ cup whipping cream

1 egg, lightly beaten

Sparkling or coarse sugar (optional)

1. Preheat oven to 375°F. Spray 9-inch square baking dish with nonstick cooking spray.

2. Combine pears, brown sugar, 2 tablespoons flour, lemon juice, 1 teaspoon ginger, cinnamon and nutmeg in large bowl; toss to coat. Spoon into prepared baking dish.

3. Combine remaining 1 cup flour, 1 teaspoon ginger, granulated sugar, baking powder and salt in medium bowl; mix well. Add butter; mix with fingertips until shaggy clumps form. Add cream and egg; stir just until combined. Drop topping, 2 tablespoonfuls at a time, into mounds over pear mixture. Sprinkle with sparkling sugar, if desired.

4. Bake 40 to 45 minutes or until filling is bubbly and topping is golden brown.

Makes 6 to 8 servings

Plum Rhubarb Crumble

1½ pounds plums, each pitted and cut into 8 wedges (4 cups)

1½ pounds rhubarb, cut into ½-inch pieces (5 cups)

1 cup granulated sugar

1 teaspoon finely grated fresh ginger

¼ teaspoon ground nutmeg

3 tablespoons cornstarch

¾ cup old-fashioned oats

½ cup all-purpose flour

½ cup packed brown sugar

½ cup sliced almonds, toasted*

¼ teaspoon salt

½ cup (1 stick) cold butter, cut into small pieces

To toast almonds, spread in single layer on ungreased baking sheet. Bake in preheated 350°F oven 5 minutes or until golden brown, stirring frequently.

1. Combine plums, rhubarb, granulated sugar, ginger and nutmeg in large bowl; toss to coat. Cover and let stand at room temperature 2 hours.

2. Preheat oven to 375°F. Spray 9-inch round or square baking dish with nonstick cooking spray. Line baking sheet with foil.

3. Pour juices from fruit mixture into small saucepan; bring to a boil over medium-high heat. Cook about 12 minutes or until reduced to syrupy consistency, stirring occasionally.* Stir in cornstarch until well blended. Stir liquid into bowl with fruit; spoon fruit mixture into prepared baking dish.

4. Combine oats, flour, brown sugar, almonds and salt in medium bowl; mix well. Add butter; mix with fingertips until butter is evenly distributed and mixture is clumpy. Sprinkle evenly over fruit mixture. Place baking dish on prepared baking sheet.

5. Bake 50 minutes or until filling is bubbly and topping is golden brown. Cool 1 hour before serving.

If fruit is not juicy after 2 hours, liquid will take less time to reduce and will require less cornstarch to thicken.

Makes 6 to 8 servings

Individual Chocolate Soufflés

1 tablespoon butter,
   plus additional
   for greasing

2 tablespoons plus
   1 teaspoon granulated
   sugar, divided

4 ounces bittersweet
   chocolate, coarsely
   chopped

2 eggs, separated, at
   room temperature

Powdered sugar
   (optional)

1. Preheat oven to 375°F. Coat two 6-ounce soufflé dishes or ramekins with butter. Add ½ teaspoon granulated sugar to each dish; shake to coat bottoms and sides.

2. Combine chocolate and 1 tablespoon butter in top of double boiler; heat over simmering water until chocolate is melted and smooth, stirring occasionally. Remove from heat; stir in egg yolks, one at a time, until blended. (Mixture may become grainy, but will smooth out with addition of egg whites.)

3. Beat egg whites in medium bowl with electric mixer at high speed until soft peaks form. Gradually add remaining 2 tablespoons granulated sugar; beat until stiff peaks form and mixture is glossy.

4. Gently fold egg whites into chocolate mixture. *Do not overmix.* (Allow some white streaks to remain.) Divide batter evenly between prepared dishes.

5. Bake 15 minutes or until soufflés rise but remain moist in centers. Sprinkle with powdered sugar, if desired. Serve immediately.

Makes 2 soufflés

Berry Peachy Cobbler

¾ cup plus 2 tablespoons all-purpose flour, divided

4 tablespoons plus 2 teaspoons sugar, divided

1¼ pounds peaches, peeled and sliced *or* 1 package (16 ounces) frozen unsweetened sliced peaches, thawed and drained

2 cups fresh raspberries *or* 1 package (12 ounces) frozen unsweetened raspberries

1 teaspoon grated lemon peel

½ teaspoon baking powder

½ teaspoon baking soda

⅛ teaspoon salt

2 tablespoons cold butter, cut into small pieces

½ cup buttermilk

1. Preheat oven to 425°F. Spray eight ramekins or 11×7-inch baking dish with nonstick cooking spray; place ramekins in jelly-roll pan or 13×9-inch baking pan.

2. Combine 2 tablespoons flour and 2 tablespoons sugar in large bowl. Add peaches, raspberries and lemon peel; toss gently to coat. Divide fruit evenly among prepared ramekins. Bake 15 minutes or until fruit is bubbly around edges.

3. Meanwhile, combine remaining ¾ cup flour, 2 tablespoons sugar, baking powder, baking soda and salt in medium bowl; mix well. Cut in butter with pastry blender or two knives until mixture resembles coarse crumbs. Stir in buttermilk just until combined.

4. Remove ramekins from oven; top fruit with equal spoonfuls of topping. Sprinkle remaining 2 teaspoons sugar over topping. Bake 18 to 20 minutes or until topping is golden brown. Serve warm.

Makes 8 servings

Bread and Butter Pudding

3 tablespoons butter, softened

1 loaf (16 ounces) egg bread or firm white bread, sliced

⅔ cup golden raisins

¾ cup sugar, divided

1 teaspoon ground cinnamon

¼ teaspoon ground nutmeg

2 cups half-and-half

2 cups whole milk

6 eggs

1½ teaspoons vanilla

1. Preheat oven to 350°F. Spray 1½-quart or 13×9-inch baking dish with nonstick cooking spray.

2. Lightly butter both sides of bread slices. Cut into 1½-inch pieces. Combine bread and raisins in prepared baking dish. Combine ¼ cup sugar, cinnamon and nutmeg in small bowl; sprinkle over bread mixture and toss to coat.

3. Whisk half-and-half, milk, eggs, remaining ½ cup sugar and vanilla in large bowl until well blended. Pour over bread mixture; let stand 10 minutes.

4. Bake about 1 hour or until pudding is set, puffed and golden brown. Serve warm or at room temperature.

Makes 8 to 10 servings

Gingered Pumpkin Custard

¾ cup sugar

2 eggs

1½ teaspoons ground cinnamon

½ teaspoon salt

½ teaspoon ground nutmeg

1 can (15 ounces) pure pumpkin

1¼ cups half-and-half

3 tablespoons finely chopped candied ginger, divided

Sweetened whipped cream (optional)

1. Preheat oven to 375°F. Place six 8-ounce ramekins or custard cups on baking sheet.

2. Combine sugar, eggs, cinnamon, salt and nutmeg in medium bowl; mix well. Add pumpkin and half-and-half; beat until well blended. Stir in 2 tablespoons ginger. Pour into prepared ramekins.

3. Bake 35 to 40 minutes or until knife inserted into centers comes out clean. Cool on wire rack at least 20 minutes before serving. Serve warm or at room temperature with whipped cream, if desired. Sprinkle with remaining 1 tablespoon ginger.

Makes 6 servings

Variation

To make one large dish of custard instead of individual servings, pour the custard mixture into a greased 8-inch or 1½-quart baking dish. Bake 45 minutes or until a knife inserted into the center comes out clean.

Baked Doughnuts with Cinnamon Glaze

2 cups milk, divided

½ cup (1 stick) butter

5 to 5½ cups all-purpose flour, divided

⅔ cup granulated sugar

2 packages (¼ ounce each) active dry yeast

1 teaspoon salt

1 teaspoon grated lemon peel

½ teaspoon ground nutmeg

2 eggs

2 cups sifted powdered sugar

½ teaspoon ground cinnamon

1. Combine 1¾ cups milk and butter in medium saucepan; heat over low heat to 120° to 130°F (butter does not need to melt completely). Combine 2 cups flour, granulated sugar, yeast, salt, lemon peel and nutmeg in large bowl of stand mixer. Gradually add milk mixture; beat with paddle attachment at low speed until blended. Beat at medium speed 2 minutes. Beat in eggs and 1 cup flour at low speed. Beat at medium speed 2 minutes.

2. Replace paddle attachment with dough hook. Mix at low speed, adding enough additional flour, about 2 cups, to form soft dough. Mix 3 minutes, adding remaining flour, 1 tablespoon at at time, if necessary to prevent sticking. Shape dough into a ball. Place dough in greased bowl; turn to grease top. Cover and refrigerate at least 2 hours or up to 24 hours.

3. Punch down dough; turn out onto lightly floured surface. Knead about 1 minute or until no longer sticky. Add enough remaining flour, 1 tablespoon at a time, if necessary to prevent sticking.

4. Line two baking sheets with parchment paper. Roll out dough to ½-inch thickness with lightly floured rolling pin. Cut out dough with floured 2½-inch doughnut cutter. Reroll scraps, reserving doughnut holes. Place doughnuts and holes 2 inches apart on prepared baking sheets. Cover and let rise in warm place about 30 minutes or until doubled in size.

5. Combine powdered sugar and cinnamon in small bowl; mix well. Stir in remaining milk, 1 tablespoon at at time, until glaze reaches desired consistency. Preheat oven to 400°F.

6. Bake doughnuts and holes 8 minutes or until golden brown. Remove to wire racks to cool 5 minutes. Place waxed paper under racks. Dip warm doughnuts into glaze; return to wire racks to set. Serve warm.

Makes 2 dozen doughnuts and holes

Tangy Cranberry Cobbler

2 cups thawed frozen or fresh cranberries

1 cup dried cranberries

1 cup raisins

½ cup orange juice

¼ cup plus 2 tablespoons sugar, divided

2 teaspoons cornstarch

1 cup all-purpose flour

2 teaspoons baking powder

1 teaspoon ground cinnamon

¼ teaspoon salt

¼ cup (½ stick) cold butter, cut into small pieces

½ cup milk

1. Preheat oven to 400°F.

2. Combine cranberries, dried cranberries, raisins, orange juice, ¼ cup sugar and cornstarch in 9-inch square or round baking dish; toss to coat.

3. Combine flour, remaining 2 tablespoons sugar, baking powder, cinnamon and salt in large bowl; mix well. Cut in butter with pastry blender or two knives until mixture resembles coarse crumbs. Add milk; stir just until combined. Drop batter by large spoonfuls over cranberry mixture.

4. Bake 35 to 40 minutes or until topping is golden brown. Serve warm.

Makes 6 servings

Oatmeal Brûlée with Raspberry Sauce

4¼ cups water, divided

½ teaspoon salt

3 cups old-fashioned oats

1 cup whipping cream

½ teaspoon vanilla

¾ cup granulated sugar, divided

3 egg yolks

6 ounces frozen sweetened raspberries

½ teaspoon orange extract

2 tablespoons packed brown sugar

1. Preheat oven to 300°F. Line baking sheet with foil. Bring 4 cups water and salt to a boil in medium saucepan over high heat. Add oats; cook over low heat 3 to 5 minutes or until water is absorbed and oats are tender, stirring occasionally. Divide oatmeal among four large ramekins or ovenproof bowls. Place ramekins on prepared baking sheet.

2. Bring cream to a simmer in small saucepan over medium heat. *Do not boil.* Remove from heat; stir in vanilla. Whisk ¼ cup granulated sugar and egg yolks in medium bowl. Slowly pour about ½ cup hot cream into egg mixture, whisking constantly. Stir egg mixture back into saucepan with cream, whisking until well blended. Pour cream mixture evenly over oatmeal in ramekins.

3. Bake 35 minutes or until almost set. Remove from oven. *Turn oven to broil.*

4. Meanwhile, prepare sauce. Combine raspberries, remaining ½ cup granulated sugar, ¼ cup water and orange extract in blender or food processor; blend until smooth. Strain sauce into bowl or pitcher.

5. Sprinkle ½ tablespoon brown sugar evenly over each custard. Broil 3 to 5 minutes or until sugar melts and browns slightly. Cool 5 to 10 minutes before serving. Serve with raspberry sauce.

Makes 4 servings

Note

This brûlée has the texture of rice pudding and the taste of sweet custard, with a crème brûlée-like topping.

Apple Blackberry Crisp

4 cups sliced peeled
   apples

Juice of ½ lemon

2 tablespoons granulated
   sugar

1 teaspoon ground
   cinnamon, divided

1 cup old-fashioned oats

6 tablespoons (¾ stick)
   cold butter, cut
   into pieces

⅔ cup packed brown
   sugar

¼ cup all-purpose flour

1 cup fresh blackberries

1. Preheat oven to 375°F. Grease 9-inch oval or 8-inch square baking dish.

2. Place apples in large bowl; drizzle with lemon juice. Add granulated sugar and ½ teaspoon cinnamon; toss to coat.

3. Combine oats, butter, brown sugar, flour and remaining ½ teaspoon cinnamon in food processor; pulse until combined, leaving some large pieces.

4. Gently stir blackberries into apple mixture. Spoon into prepared baking dish; sprinkle with oat mixture.

5. Bake 30 to 40 minutes or until filling is bubbly and topping is golden brown.

Makes 6 servings

Variation

This crisp can also be made without the blackberries; just add an additional 1 cup sliced apples.

Panettone Bread Pudding

½ (2-pound) loaf panettone bread, cut into ¾-inch cubes (8 cups)

6 eggs

½ cup sugar

3 cups half-and-half

1 teaspoon vanilla

½ teaspoon ground cinnamon

¼ teaspoon salt

Powdered sugar

Caramel sauce or ice cream topping (optional)

1. Preheat oven to 350°F. Spray 11×7-inch baking dish with nonstick cooking spray.

2. Arrange bread cubes in prepared baking dish. Whisk eggs and sugar in large bowl until blended. Add half-and-half, vanilla, cinnamon and salt; whisk until well blended. Pour mixture over bread, pressing down to moisten top. Let stand 15 minutes.

3. Bake 40 to 45 minutes or until puffed and golden brown. Serve warm or at room temperature. Sprinkle with powdered sugar; serve with caramel sauce, if desired.

Makes 12 servings

Plum Cobbler with Cinnamon Drop Biscuits

6   cups sliced ripe plums
    (about 12 medium)

1   cup plus 2 tablespoons
    all-purpose flour,
    divided

8   tablespoons granulated
    sugar, divided

¼   cup packed brown
    sugar

1   tablespoon lemon juice

2   teaspoons baking
    powder

½   teaspoon ground
    cinnamon

¼   teaspoon salt

¼   cup (½ stick) cold
    butter, cut into
    small pieces

8   to 10 tablespoons milk

1. Preheat oven to 400°F. Spray 8-inch square baking dish with nonstick cooking spray.

2. Combine plums, 2 tablespoons flour, 6 tablespoons granulated sugar, brown sugar and lemon juice in large bowl; toss to coat. Spoon into prepared baking dish. Bake 10 minutes.

3. Meanwhile, combine remaining 1 cup flour, 2 tablespoons granulated sugar, baking powder, cinnamon and salt in medium bowl; mix well. Cut in butter with pastry blender or two knives until mixture resembles coarse crumbs. Add milk, 1 tablespoon at a time, stirring until sticky dough forms. Drop heaping tablespoonfuls of dough over plum mixture.

4. Bake 20 minutes or until golden brown. Serve warm.

Makes 6 servings

Apple Cranberry Crumble

4 large apples (about 1⅓ pounds), peeled and cut into ¼-inch slices

2 cups fresh or frozen cranberries

⅓ cup granulated sugar

6 tablespoons all-purpose flour, divided

1 teaspoon apple pie spice, divided

¼ teaspoon salt, divided

½ cup chopped walnuts

¼ cup old-fashioned oats

2 tablespoons packed brown sugar

¼ cup (½ stick) butter, cut into small pieces

1. Preheat oven to 375°F.

2. Combine apples, cranberries, granulated sugar, 2 tablespoons flour, ½ teaspoon apple pie spice and ⅛ teaspoon salt in large bowl; toss to coat. Spoon into medium (8-inch) ovenproof skillet.

3. Combine remaining 4 tablespoons flour, ½ teaspoon apple pie spice, ⅛ teaspoon salt, walnuts, oats and brown sugar in medium bowl; mix well. Cut in butter with pastry blender or two knives until mixture resembles coarse crumbs. Sprinkle over fruit mixture in skillet.

4. Bake 50 to 60 minutes or until filling is bubbly and topping is lightly browned.

Makes 4 servings

Shortcut Baking

Quicker Pecan Pie

½ (16-ounce) package
　　refrigerated sugar
　　cookie dough

¼ cup all-purpose flour

3 eggs

¾ cup dark corn syrup

¾ cup sugar

1 teaspoon vanilla

¼ teaspoon salt

2 cups chopped pecans

1. Preheat oven to 350°F. Lightly spray 9-inch pie plate with nonstick cooking spray. Let dough stand at room temperature 15 minutes.

2. Combine cookie dough and flour in large bowl; mix well. Press dough evenly onto bottom and ½ inch up side of prepared pie plate. Crimp edge with fork. Bake 20 minutes.

3. Meanwhile, beat eggs in large bowl. Add corn syrup, sugar, vanilla and salt; beat until well blended. Pour into crust; sprinkle evenly with pecans.

4. Bake 40 to 45 minutes or just until center is set. Cool completely on wire rack.

Makes 8 servings

Orange Cinnamon Rolls

½ cup packed brown sugar

3 tablespoons butter, melted, divided

1 tablespoon ground cinnamon

1 teaspoon grated orange peel

1 loaf (16 ounces) frozen bread dough, thawed according to package directions

⅓ cup raisins (optional)

1 to 2 tablespoons orange juice

½ cup powdered sugar, sifted

1. Spray two 8-inch round cake pans with nonstick cooking spray. Combine brown sugar, 1 tablespoon butter, cinnamon and orange peel in small bowl; mix well.

2. Roll out dough into 18×8-inch rectangle on lightly floured surface. Brush remaining 2 tablespoons butter over dough; sprinkle evenly with brown sugar mixture. Sprinkle with raisins, if desired.

3. Starting with long side, roll up dough jelly-roll style; pinch seam to seal. Cut crosswise into 1-inch slices; arrange slices cut sides down in prepared pans. Cover loosely with plastic wrap; let rise in warm place 30 to 40 minutes or until almost doubled in size. Preheat oven to 350°F.

4. Bake 18 minutes or until golden brown. Immediately remove to wire racks; cool slightly.

5. Stir orange juice into powdered sugar in small bowl until smooth and consistency is thin enough to pour. Drizzle glaze over warm rolls.

Makes 18 rolls

Rosemary Parmesan Biscuit Poppers

2¼ cups biscuit baking mix

⅔ cup milk

⅓ cup grated Parmesan cheese, divided

1 tablespoon chopped fresh rosemary *or* 1 teaspoon dried rosemary, crumbled

⅛ teaspoon ground red pepper

3 tablespoons extra virgin olive oil

⅛ to ¼ teaspoon coarse salt or sea salt (optional)

1. Preheat oven to 450°F. Line large baking sheet with parchment paper or spray with nonstick cooking spray.

2. Combine biscuit mix, milk, ¼ cup cheese, rosemary and red pepper in medium bowl; mix well.

3. Drop dough by teaspoonfuls in 1-inch mounds onto prepared baking sheet. Sprinkle with remaining cheese.

4. Bake 8 to 10 minutes or until golden brown. Brush biscuits with oil; sprinkle with salt, if desired. Serve immediately.

Makes 24 small biscuits

Spanikopita Pull-Aparts

- 4 tablespoons (½ stick) butter, melted, divided
- 12 frozen white dinner rolls (⅓ of 3-pound package),* thawed according to package directions
- 1 package (10 ounces) frozen chopped spinach, thawed and squeezed dry
- 4 green onions, finely chopped (about ¼ cup packed)
- 1 clove garlic, minced
- 1 teaspoon dried dill weed
- ½ teaspoon salt
- ⅛ teaspoon black pepper
- 1 cup (4 ounces) crumbled feta cheese
- ¾ cup (3 ounces) grated Monterey Jack cheese, divided

If frozen dinner rolls are not available, substitute one 16-ounce loaf of frozen bread dough or pizza dough. Thaw according to package directions and divide into 12 pieces.

1. Brush large (10-inch) ovenproof skillet with ½ tablespoon butter. Cut rolls in half to make 24 balls of dough.

2. Combine spinach, green onions, garlic, dill weed, salt and pepper in medium bowl; mix well to break apart spinach. Add feta, ½ cup Monterey Jack and remaining 3½ tablespoons butter; mix well.

3. Coat each ball of dough with spinach mixture; arrange in single layer in prepared skillet. Sprinkle any remaining spinach mixture over and between balls of dough. Cover and let rise in warm place about 40 minutes or until almost doubled in size. Preheat oven to 350°F. Sprinkle remaining ¼ cup Monterey Jack over dough.

4. Bake 35 to 40 minutes or until golden brown. Serve warm.

Makes 24 rolls

Apple Pie Pockets

2 pieces lavash bread, each cut into 4 rectangles

2 tablespoons melted butter

¾ cup apple pie filling

1 egg, lightly beaten with 1 teaspoon water

½ cup powdered sugar

⅛ teaspoon ground cinnamon

2½ teaspoons milk

1. Preheat oven to 400°F. Line baking sheet with parchment paper.

2. Brush one side of each piece of lavash with butter. Place half of lavash pieces buttered-side down on work surface. Spoon 3 tablespoons pie filling in center of each piece, leaving ½-inch border. Brush border with egg mixture; top with remaining lavash pieces, buttered-side up. Press edges together with fork to seal.

3. Use paring knife to cut three small slits in center of each pocket. Place on prepared baking sheet.

4. Bake 18 minutes or until crust is golden and crisp. Remove to wire rack to cool 15 minutes.

5. Combine powdered sugar and cinnamon in small bowl; stir in milk until smooth. Drizzle glaze over pockets; let stand 15 minutes to set.

Makes 4 servings

Easy Cheesy Bubble Loaf

2 packages (12 ounces each) refrigerated buttermilk biscuits (10 biscuits per package)

2 tablespoons butter, melted

1½ cups (6 ounces) shredded Italian cheese blend

1. Preheat oven to 350°F. Spray 9×5-inch loaf pan with nonstick cooking spray.

2. Separate biscuits; cut each biscuit into four pieces with scissors. Layer half of biscuit pieces in prepared pan. Drizzle with 1 tablespoon butter; sprinkle with 1 cup cheese. Top with remaining biscuit pieces, 1 tablespoon butter and ½ cup cheese.

3. Bake about 25 minutes or until golden brown. Serve warm.

Makes 12 servings

Tip

It's easy to change up the flavors in this simple bread. Try Mexican cheese blend instead of Italian, and add taco seasoning and/or hot pepper sauce to the melted butter before drizzling it over the dough. Or, sprinkle ¼ cup chopped ham, salami or crumbled crisp-cooked bacon between the layers of dough.

BBQ Chicken Flatbread

3 tablespoons red wine vinegar

2 teaspoons sugar

¼ red onion, thinly sliced (about ⅓ cup)

3 cups shredded rotisserie chicken

½ cup barbecue sauce

1 package (about 14 ounces) refrigerated pizza dough

All-purpose flour, for dusting

1½ cups (6 ounces) shredded mozzarella cheese

1 green onion, thinly sliced diagonally

2 tablespoons chopped fresh cilantro

1. Preheat oven to 400°F. Line baking sheet with parchment paper.

2. Combine vinegar and sugar in small bowl; stir until sugar is dissolved. Add red onion; cover and let stand at room temperature while preparing flatbread.

3. Combine chicken and barbecue sauce in medium bowl; toss to coat.

4. Roll out dough into 11×9-inch rectangle on lightly floured surface. Transfer dough to prepared baking sheet; top with cheese and barbecue chicken mixture.

5. Bake about 12 minutes or until crust is golden brown and cheese is melted. Drain red onion. Sprinkle red onion, green onion and cilantro over flatbread. Serve immediately.

Makes 4 servings

Breakfast Sausage Monkey Muffins

8 ounces bulk pork
  sausage

1 egg, beaten

1 cup (4 ounces)
  shredded Mexican
  cheese blend, divided

1 package (12 ounces)
  refrigerated
  buttermilk biscuits
  (10 biscuits)

1. Preheat oven to 350°F. Spray 8 standard (2½-inch) muffin cups with nonstick cooking spray.

2. Cook and stir sausage in large skillet over medium-high heat about 8 minutes or until no longer pink, breaking apart any large pieces. Spoon sausage and drippings into large bowl; let cool 2 minutes. Add egg; stir until blended. Reserve 2 tablespoons cheese for tops of muffins; stir remaining cheese into sausage mixture.

3. Separate biscuits; cut each biscuit into six pieces with scissors. Roll biscuit pieces in sausage mixture to coat; place seven to eight biscuit pieces in each muffin cup. Sprinkle with reserved 2 tablespoons cheese.

4. Bake about 22 minutes or until golden brown. Remove muffins to paper towel-lined plate. Serve warm.

Makes 8 muffins

Pesto Parmesan Twists

1 loaf (16 ounces) frozen bread dough, thawed according to package directions

¼ cup pesto sauce

⅔ cup grated Parmesan cheese, divided

1 tablespoon olive oil

1. Line baking sheets with parchment paper.

2. Roll out dough into 20×10-inch rectangle on lightly floured surface. Spread pesto evenly over half of dough; sprinkle with ⅓ cup cheese. Fold remaining half of dough over filling, forming 10-inch square.

3. Roll square into 12×10-inch rectangle. Cut into 12 (1-inch) strips with sharp knife. Cut strips in half crosswise to form 24 strips total. Twist each strip several times; place on prepared baking sheets. Cover with plastic wrap; let rise in warm place 20 minutes.

4. Preheat oven to 350°F. Brush breadsticks with oil; sprinkle with remaining ⅓ cup cheese.

5. Bake 16 to 18 minutes or until golden brown. Serve warm.

Makes 24 breadsticks

Quick Chocolate Chip Sticky Buns

2 tablespoons butter

1 package (11 ounces) refrigerated French bread dough

¼ cup sugar

1 teaspoon ground cinnamon

½ cup mini semisweet chocolate chips

⅓ cup pecan pieces, toasted*

1 tablespoon maple syrup

To toast pecans, spread on ungreased baking sheet. Bake in preheated 350°F oven 6 to 8 minutes or until golden brown, stirring frequently.

1. Preheat oven to 350°F. Place butter in 9-inch round cake pan; place pan in oven while preheating to melt butter.

2. Meanwhile, unroll dough on cutting board or clean work surface. Combine sugar and cinnamon in small bowl; sprinkle evenly over dough. Top with chocolate chips. Starting with short side, roll up dough jelly-roll style. Cut crosswise into eight slices with serrated knife.

3. Remove pan from oven. Stir pecans and maple syrup into melted butter; mix well. Place dough slices cut sides up in pan, pressing gently into pecan mixture.

4. Bake 20 to 22 minutes or until golden brown. Immediately invert pan onto serving plate; scrape any pecans or butter mixture remaining in pan over buns. Serve warm.

Makes 8 sticky buns

Barbecue Cauliflower Calzones

1 head cauliflower,
   cut into florets
   and thinly sliced

2 tablespoons olive oil

   Salt and black pepper

¾ cup barbecue sauce

1 package (about
   14 ounces) refrigerated
   pizza dough

½ medium onion, chopped

1 cup (4 ounces)
   shredded mozzarella
   cheese

   Ranch or blue cheese
   dressing

1. Preheat oven to 400°F.

2. Place cauliflower on baking sheet. Drizzle with oil and season lightly with salt and pepper; toss to coat. Spread in single layer.

3. Roast 30 minutes or until cauliflower is browned and very tender, stirring once. Transfer to medium bowl; stir in barbecue sauce.

4. Unroll dough on cutting board. Stretch into 11×17-inch rectangle; cut into quarters. Place one fourth of onion on half of each piece of dough. Top with one fourth of cauliflower and ¼ cup cheese. Fold dough over filling; roll and pinch edges to seal. Place on baking sheet. Spray with nonstick cooking spray or brush with oil to help crust brown.

5. Bake 10 minutes or until golden brown. Serve with ranch dressing.

Makes 4 servings

Apple Pie Monkey Bread

½ cup (1 stick) butter, divided

2 large apples (about 1 pound), peeled and cut into ½-inch pieces (Fuji, Granny Smith or Braeburn)

½ cup plus 1 tablespoon sugar, divided

2½ teaspoons ground cinnamon, divided

½ cup finely chopped pecans

2 packages (12 ounces each) refrigerated buttermilk biscuits (10 biscuits per package)

1. Preheat oven to 350°F. Spray 9-inch deep-dish pie plate with nonstick cooking spray.

2. Melt ¼ cup butter in large skillet or saucepan over medium heat. Add apples, 1 tablespoon sugar and ½ teaspoon cinnamon; cook and stir 5 minutes or until apples are tender and glazed. Transfer to large bowl. Melt remaining ¼ cup butter in same skillet, stirring to scrape up any glaze. Cool slightly.

3. Combine pecans, remaining ½ cup sugar and 2 teaspoons cinnamon in medium bowl. Separate biscuits; cut each biscuit into four pieces with scissors. Dip biscuit pieces in melted butter; roll in pecan mixture to coat. Place one fourth of biscuit pieces in prepared pie plate; top with one fourth of apples. Repeat layers three times. Sprinkle with remaining pecan mixture and drizzle with any remaining butter.

4. Bake 30 minutes or until biscuits are firm and topping is golden brown. Serve warm.

Makes about 12 servings

Skillet Cinnamon Pecan Rolls

4 tablespoons (½ stick) butter, melted, divided

1 loaf (16 ounces) frozen bread dough, thawed according to package directions

½ cup packed dark brown sugar

2 teaspoons ground cinnamon

½ cup chopped pecans

1. Brush large (10-inch) ovenproof skillet with ½ tablespoon melted butter. Roll out dough into 18×8-inch rectangle on lightly floured surface.

2. Combine brown sugar, 3 tablespoons butter and cinnamon in medium bowl; mix well. Brush mixture evenly over dough; sprinkle with pecans. Starting with long side, roll up dough jelly-roll style; pinch seam to seal.

3. Cut crosswise into 1-inch slices; arrange slices cut sides up in prepared skillet. Cover loosely and let rise in warm place about 30 minutes or until doubled in size. Preheat oven to 350°F.

4. Brush tops of rolls with remaining ½ tablespoon butter. Bake 20 to 25 minutes or until golden brown. Serve warm.

Makes about 18 rolls

Pepperoni Pizza Biscuits

2 cups biscuit baking mix

½ teaspoon Italian seasoning

2 tablespoons cold butter, cut into thin slices

⅔ cup milk

½ cup finely chopped pepperoni

¼ cup finely chopped drained oil-packed sun-dried tomatoes

½ cup (2 ounces) shredded Italian cheese blend

1. Preheat oven to 425°F. Line baking sheet with parchment paper or spray with nonstick cooking spray.

2. Combine biscuit mix and Italian seasoning in large bowl; mix well. Cut in butter with pastry blender or two knives until mixture resembles coarse crumbs. Gradually stir in milk, adding enough to form slightly sticky dough. Gently stir in pepperoni and sun-dried tomatoes.

3. Turn dough out onto lightly floured surface; pat to ¾-inch thickness. Cut out biscuits with 2½-inch biscuit or cookie cutter. Place 1 inch apart on prepared baking sheet; pat 1 tablespoon cheese on each biscuit.

4. Bake 15 to 18 minutes or until golden brown. Remove to wire rack to cool.

Makes 8 biscuits

Metric Conversion Chart

VOLUME MEASUREMENTS (dry)

1/8 teaspoon	= 0.5 mL
1/4 teaspoon	= 1 mL
1/2 teaspoon	= 2 mL
3/4 teaspoon	= 4 mL
1 teaspoon	= 5 mL
1 tablespoon	= 15 mL
2 tablespoons	= 30 mL
1/4 cup	= 60 mL
1/3 cup	= 75 mL
1/2 cup	= 125 mL
2/3 cup	= 150 mL
3/4 cup	= 175 mL
1 cup	= 250 mL
2 cups = 1 pint	= 500 mL
3 cups	= 750 mL
4 cups = 1 quart	= 1 L

VOLUME MEASUREMENTS (fluid)

1 fluid ounce (2 tablespoons) = 30 mL
4 fluid ounces (1/2 cup) = 125 mL
8 fluid ounces (1 cup) = 250 mL
12 fluid ounces (1 1/2 cups) = 375 mL
16 fluid ounces (2 cups) = 500 mL

WEIGHTS (mass)

1/2 ounce	= 15 g
1 ounce	= 30 g
3 ounces	= 90 g
4 ounces	= 120 g
8 ounces	= 225 g
10 ounces	= 285 g
12 ounces	= 360 g
16 ounces = 1 pound	= 450 g

DIMENSIONS

1/16 inch	= 2 mm
1/8 inch	= 3 mm
1/4 inch	= 6 mm
1/2 inch	= 1.5 cm
3/4 inch	= 2 cm
1 inch	= 2.5 cm

OVEN TEMPERATURES

250°F	= 120°C
275°F	= 140°C
300°F	= 150°C
325°F	= 160°C
350°F	= 180°C
375°F	= 190°C
400°F	= 200°C
425°F	= 220°C
450°F	= 230°C

BAKING PAN SIZES

Utensil	Size in Inches/Quarts	Metric Volume	Size in Centimeters
Baking or Cake Pan (square or rectangular)	8×8×2	2 L	20×20×5
	9×9×2	2.5 L	23×23×5
	12×8×2	3 L	30×20×5
	13×9×2	3.5 L	33×23×5
Loaf Pan	8×4×3	1.5 L	20×10×7
	9×5×3	2 L	23×13×7
Round Layer Cake Pan	8×1½	1.2 L	20×4
	9×1½	1.5 L	23×4
Pie Plate	8×1¼	750 mL	20×3
	9×1¼	1 L	23×3
Baking Dish or Casserole	1 quart	1 L	—
	1½ quart	1.5 L	—
	2 quart	2 L	—